Ctrl
Alt
Delete

Also by Mitch Joel

SIX PIXELS OF SEPARATION:
Everyone Is Connected. Connect Your Business to Everyone.

Ctrl Alt Delete

Reboot Your Business. Reboot Your Life. Your Future Depends on It.

Mitch Joel
President of Twist Image
Author of *Six Pixels of Separation*

BUSINESS PLUS

NEW YORK   BOSTON

Business Plus

Hachette Book Group

237 Park Avenue

New York, NY 10017

www.HachetteBookGroup.com

Printed in the United States of America

RRD-C

First Edition: May 2013

10 9 8 7 6 5 4 3 2 1

Business Plus is an imprint of Grand Central Publishing.
The Business Plus name and logo are trademarks of Hachette Book Group, Inc.

The Hachette Speakers Bureau provides a wide range of authors for speaking events. To find out more, go to www.hachettespeakersbureau.com or call (866) 376-6591.

The publisher is not responsible for websites (or their content) that are not owned by the publisher.

Library of Congress Cataloging-in-Publication Data

Joel, Mitch.

Ctrl alt delete : reboot your business. reboot your life. your future depends on it / Mitch Joel, President of Twist Image, author of Six Pixels of Separation.

pages cm

Includes index.

ISBN 978-1-4555-2330-6 (hbk.)—ISBN 978-1-4555-2331-3 (ebk.)—ISBN 978-1-61969-378-4 (audiobook)

1. Electronic commerce.   2. Business enterprises—Computer networks.
3. Internet marketing.   4. Entrepreneurship.   I. Title.

HF5548.32.J64 2013

658.8'72—dc23

2012040770

ISBN 978-1-4555-4548-3 (international edition)

#forever

This book is dedicated to Ali, Julien, and Sophie . . . the only part of my life that never requires a reboot or a desire to squiggle. I love you and cherish you through each and every day. Every moment and with every breath, you are my everything.

Contents

SECTION 2 *Reboot: You*

Ctrl
Alt
Delete

Prelude

The next time you attend a conference, I want you to look to your left and then to your right.

In the next five years, odds are that one out of three of you won't be around. When I speak to audiences all over the world, this is the message of "hope" that I deliver. And yes, it is a message of hope. This is a time of great upheaval in business. You know it, and you see it every day. In fact, the argument could be made that this is the first time—in the history of business—when consumers are fundamentally ahead of the brands that serve them. Consumers are more connected, more informed, creating and sharing more. They're smart and getting smarter.

The challenge is that most businesses don't know how to adapt, and most of the people who are working for these companies don't know how to change their old ways. Technology hasn't just transformed how we buy or sell our wares to consumers or how we connect socially. Technology has sent business through a rapid state of genetic mutation, and we're still in the middle of this evolution. I call this moment in time the following: purgatory. We're not in hell . . . but this certainly isn't heaven either.

Ctrl Alt Delete is intended to both clear the brush and act as your road map through this purgatory. The truth is that many are scared because they don't know what to do, while many others see this as one of the best opportunities they will have in their professional lifetimes. This isn't about simple semantics and shifting your mindset or doing a slight reorg of your company; it's about understanding that during this state of purgatory many businesses will die and many jobs will disappear, but in the same breath many businesses will thrive, many new businesses will be created, and many new jobs will be invented.

The only question this book will truly answer is: Do you want to be employable in the next five years?

THIS COULD BE ANYONE'S STORY...

The neighbors downstairs have had enough. They're thinking about complaining to the cops about the constant noise. Who runs a business out of their apartment? Is that even legal? The constant hum of music, the muted bumps from the Embody office chair as it rolls across the floor, and the 3:32 a.m. sounds from the gourmet coffee machine.

Oh, and let's not forget about the heated debates that creep through the walls of the apartment and seep into the neighbors' space—the conversations that seem to increase in volume and frustration when the video Skype call fails. Why doesn't this guy just go to an office during the day like the rest of us?

THIS IS THE STORY OF MARCO ARMENT...

Marco Arment is changing the face of business forever with his computer, smartphone, home office, and one new user after another.

What does the near future of business look like? If Arment has anything to do with it, it may well look like his Manhattan apartment. Arment had it all and tossed it all away for something else. He was the co-founder and chief technology officer at tumblr—one of the hottest online social networking sites. Many digerati see the growing popularity of tumblr as the next big thing. Tumblr could be the next Facebook...or Twitter...or YouTube...or who knows?

But Arment gave it all up. While working on tumblr, Arment constantly grappled with bookmarking applications and printed articles from the Web. Instead of finding a solution that worked for him as a better way to keep all of this information organized and readily available, Arment quit tumblr to build the product for himself. Anyone who uses a computer, smartphone, and tablet in combination or solo should probably be using Arment's creation: Instapaper. With over one million registered users (a quarter of whom use it on a regular basis), Instapaper makes it incredibly easy to save articles that can be read and synchronized on any other computer, smartphone, or tablet. It's not a website. Instapaper is just a simple little application. It can run in your Web browser's toolbar, or you can download the app to your smartphone of choice.

The concept for Instapaper—and its rapid ascent—makes it worth millions. At this point, it's hard to tell what the true valuation would be, because Arment has fully self-funded the service and acts as the sole employee. The only real question is this: *If a multimillion-dollar business can be developed and managed by one person with a laptop in an apartment, what happens to your business and your job as this rapid innovation and digitization continues to ripple through every industry?*

There is a startling realization in Arment's story: There's a good chance that your current business (or job) may not even be around in the next five years. Wacky prediction? Marketing hype to sell a book? It isn't. Arment's story isn't an anomaly. Did you ever think it was even possible to have a one-person company with well over one million customers and a multimillion-dollar valuation?

Welcome to purgatory (or heaven, if you're Marco Arment).

Apple co-founder and former CEO Steve Jobs once said, "If you don't cannibalize yourself, someone else will." That's what Arment did...that's what you need to start thinking about as well—whether it's your job, your business, or your career.

RIGHT HERE, RIGHT NOW.

Ctrl Alt Delete is written to provide the road map for your business and the triggers (or attitudinal habits) that you will need to work within (and through) this massive and constant transformation that is happening in our post-disruption world. The fallout is going to be very bleak for many businesses. With that comes massive opportunity for the companies and individuals who are brave enough to see this as an once-in-a-lifetime chance to do something amazing with their lives. Yes, this book will help you become amazing.

Ctrl Alt Delete will teach you how to identify these opportunities and how to seize them. It will show you how to transform your thinking for this very different business world, and it will act as your guide on the path through purgatory toward redemption and the Promised Land. This book will enable you to both see the trends and evaluate the new business opportunities that await you. *Ctrl Alt Delete* is about how you should be thinking and navigating your business through this time of purgatory. Remember how I asked at the beginning of this book to look to your left...and then to your right. In the next five years, there's a strong likelihood that at least one of your major competitors won't make it through this transformation. It might even be you. Please, don't let it be you.

Introduction

Ctrl Alt Delete is broken into two sections. The first half ("Reboot: Business") is about how we're going to embrace this dramatic reset of business. In this section, we'll look at five major movements that are converging and how they will require businesses and the people who serve them to adapt like never before. In the second part of the book ("Reboot: You"), we're going to get personal and talk about you. The fact is that not only will we need to understand these five major movements, but we'll also have to reboot who we are and how we work. I have uncovered seven triggers that will help you (and the people you work with) transition from being a "jobber" (someone working nine-to-five, clock-watching, and waiting on your pension plan) to someone who is doing the work that you were meant to accomplish. That's the real big idea here: The future of business isn't about what's written in a contract, it's about what we do with every waking moment to make it count. These triggers apply to entrepreneurs or being an entrepreneur within an existing organization. You're going to have to figure out what you want to be, because the future of business will be predicated on these new types of workers.

Why a book about this? Businesses and the people who work

for them no longer have a choice. They must reboot. They must Ctrl Alt Delete. What we're currently seeing in the marketplace is the struggle that businesses and employees are going through as we live through this state of purgatory. We are stuck in the middle of this transition and digitization of industry, and we've had enough of the analysis paralysis that is grabbing businesses by the throat. What we need—more than anything else—are the insights and guidance that will be crucial to our success. These insights and guidance are what *Ctrl Alt Delete* is all about. It's a road map for business and professional success moving forward.

Pundits will tell you that social media has changed everything. Fine. In the immortal words of a snarky sixteen-year-old girl, "Whatever...get over it!" *Ctrl Alt Delete* moves forward with this one thought: *Now what?*

SECTION 1

REBOOT: BUSINESS

CHAPTER 1

From Me to You

The shift toward direct relationships with consumers.

Several years ago a leading brand (that shall remain nameless) contacted my marketing agency, Twist Image, about a new business opportunity in the digital space. The brand's reality was this: As the years passed by, they were discovering that the number of retailers they were selling to was diminishing at a rapid and terrifying pace.

As the major big-box outlets continue to grow and as consolidation rifles through the retail sector, the bigger brands have only a handful of outlets to sell their wares. Plus, with these retailers' size and growth comes another reality: They begin to dictate everything from quantity and terms to acceptable margins. For some businesses, this is a dream come true because it secures significant sales, but for others (like this brand), a massive global business was becoming a game of diminishing returns. They were selling to fewer stores at weakening margins. It got ugly fast if you ran the numbers: Eventually this brand would only have their products on the shelves of one or two of the major retailers, which would be constantly dictating and changing the terms of sale. Beyond that came the retailers' demands for either exclusivity, their own unique product lines, or both. At the end of the day, the brand/

client came to a harsh realization: While they were a household name, they had no direct relationship with the consumer.

HOW DO YOU WIN?

The client's idea was to create a new e-commerce brand online that housed only their own brand-name products but would feel like a new online player. This was their last chance. While they constantly battled with retailers over the rights to sell their own products directly to consumers online, the time had come to draw a line in the sand. This project became the hope and prayer to save the business. They would use this online business as a place to start a direct relationship with the consumer.

Notwithstanding how the major retailers might have felt about this project—in terms of how it would not only cannibalize their business but perhaps keep customers away—it would have been a very smart and wise play for the brand to make. For a brand to truly shape its own destiny, it must lead the relationship with the consumer as well. I was fully behind this initiative...so what happened? The company never pulled the trigger on their e-commerce project, and now they're busy scrambling for "likes" on Facebook and are selling their products through the handful of big-box retailers left. Ironically, other, scrappier startups have disrupted this traditional retail model with digital-only brands that are capturing the imagination (and money) of consumers all over the world.

WHAT APPLE KNOWS.

What happened prior to 2001 that made Apple go into the retail business? Whenever the topic of Apple and the Apple retail experience (aka Apple Store) is brought up, many media pundits roll their eyes as if the success of these sparse and crisp stores is some kind of anomaly in business lore. It's not. Apple came to a conclusion in the 1990s that many businesses have yet to wake up to. They knew that if potential customers walked into a traditional consumer electronics goods store and became inundated with a massive selection of computers and laptops, they would, instinctively, defer to the first sales associate they could wrestle down. What would happen next? Would the sales associates spend the time needed to uncover the needs of individual customers, or would they attempt to sell those same customers whatever was either on sale or would garner them the highest commission? I think we all know the answer to that question.

The solution for Apple was to create a "cradle to the grave" business model where the customer is—at every touch point—speaking directly with Apple's brand. A true, direct relationship—in every sense of the word. Apple could not win on price (their computers and other devices are usually much more expensive than their competition's), so they had to win by being there for the consumer and by making these consumers a part of a more complete brand ecosystem. Don't think for a second that the Genius Bar doesn't play directly into this very forward-thinking business strategy, which is driven by the power of direct relationships.

At the time that Apple first launched retail stores in 2001, the common practice among retailers was to cram each nook and cranny of space with merchandise to maximize the sales per square foot. Sadly, most retailers (and businesses) still hold on to this traditional thinking. For Apple, it was less about every square foot of retail space and much more about every square inch of the direct relationship. Apple didn't start in the retail business to compete with other consumer electronics stores; they went into retail for the direct relationship with their customers. Apple's attitude was: "Why give that power to Best Buy or anyone else?"

HOW ARE YOUR DIRECT RELATIONSHIPS?

Some brands do this well . . . but most fail at it in spectacular fashion. Is it possible to be so judgmental? It is. One of the reasons I still enjoy the debate about the efficacy of social media marketing is that the majority of brands that struggle with the return on investment are comparing it with traditional push advertising, instead of treating it as an opportunity to have real interactions between real people (one of the core pillars of my first book, *Six Pixels of Separation*). A consumer who hits a "like" or "follow" button is opening up the perfect opportunity to have a direct relationship with a brand. If all the brand does is blast back impersonal offers and specials, it is simply not pushing toward direct relationships . . . it's pushing toward broadcast advertising.

THIS ISN'T ABOUT SOCIAL MEDIA (ANYMORE) . . . IT'S ABOUT MAKING YOUR BUSINESS MORE SOCIAL.

This is a very unique moment in time. It is not only a revolution in business—one that we will probably never again see in our lifetimes—but it is ours either to capitalize on or to squander. The truth is that most businesses are wasting this moment because they are unable to think and react through this purgatory. The next five years are going to be about these direct relationships. The next five years are going to be about how well a brand can actually change a relationship from one that looks at how many people are in their database (and how to target them more effectively with advertising messages) . . . to one focusing on precisely who those individuals are and how the brand can make the connection with them even stronger.

THE STARS ARE ALIGNED.

We have the technology. We have the data. We have the new media channels and platforms. We have the opportunity to publish whatever we want—in text, images, audio, and video—instantly (and for free) to the world. What we do with this moment will be telling. It will also set the pace for everything that flows out of our businesses for the next decade.

NO DIRECT RELATIONSHIPS. NO FUTURE.

The true opportunity going forward is for your business to develop a direct relationship with your consumers. But there's a big challenge to this. It turns out that your competition is no longer just your traditional competitors, because suddenly joining the fray are your third-party resellers or anyone else who sells your products on your behalf. Confused? You should be.

The official Beats By Dre Facebook page has over five million people who have liked it (as of this writing). You can buy your Dre Beats Solo Headphones with ControlTalk from Target for about $180. Target has over twenty million likes on their Facebook page. Both Target and Beats By Dre are actively amping up their likes on Facebook. It's not a subtle, sit-back-and-relax type of play. They are both enthusiastically and actively fighting for every like and friend they can find (one aspect of direct relationship building).

What's a confused consumer to do? If I bought my Beats By Dre at Target, am I supposed to like the Beats By Dre Facebook page? The Target Facebook page? Both? The answer is: I don't know . . . and that's the problem. To add to this confusion and complexity, we also can't ignore Facebook.

With well over a billion users, Facebook is an Internet unto itself. Not unlike other online social networks, there is a cost to being active on Facebook, and that cost is both the data and the direct relationship with your consumers. While Facebook continues to work more closely with businesses to help build this engagement, much like Las Vegas, what happens on Facebook *stays* on Facebook. If you have three thousand people who like your brand on Facebook, you can't pick them up (with all of their data, usage, and engagement) and take them over to your website.

In essence, Facebook actually owns the direct relationship with the consumer here; you're merely on their turf leveraging the consumer's activity. The Facebook value proposition to Wall Street is simple: We *own* the data and direct relationships with these hundreds of millions of people, and the value is in the data and the ability to put advertising on the pages of content that these people are creating and sharing (more on that in chapter 2).

And it's not just Facebook—it's everyone who allows you access to an audience online. If you're posting videos to YouTube and are lucky enough to be generating millions of views and positive reviews, what would happen if you suddenly started posting the videos only to your website? Where does the true community reside? While your company may be able to lure some of its audience over for a new video (or two), you will quickly come to the realization that YouTube is where the activity is. That is where the direct relationship lives.

You can see that it's a real horse race for that key direct relationship: There's your company; there are the clients that you sell through (or your value-added partnerships); there are the channels and platforms that you're engaging through...and we still haven't even made our way down the competitive food chain to your true competitors.

CONSUMER-CENTRIC CAN'T JUST BE YOUR BUSINESS JARGON.

The best way to begin thinking about these direct relationships is to reboot your perspective. In the past year, I've shifted my presentations on digital media. I've moved them away (almost completely) from what businesses should be doing in the digital marketing space to focusing them 100 percent on what customers are actually doing—out in the wild. Don't misconstrue the term *customer-focused* to mean that I really care about the consumer (this is the traditional way of looking at business). Customer-focused in 2013 means looking at things as a consumer and not as a businessperson. It may sound overly simplified, but how we think about business during regular working hours is usually diametrically opposed to how we act as consumers. We'll instinctively ask in a boardroom, "Does anyone really download and use apps on their iPhone?," and later that week we'll spend our hard-earned dollars downloading apps and content to our smartphones. Instead, we should think like our true customers. We should start acting like them. Sadly, most brands are not thinking like their customers. Don't believe me? When you wake up in the morning, what's the first thing you grab? How long is it before you grab your iPhone? And yet most brands are still doing little to embrace this new consumer.

WHAT'S YOUR BUSINESS REALLY UP TO?

Your business needs to not only sense this urgency, but also realize this seismic shift in the battle for direct relationships. While some businesses are beginning to capitalize on this by recognizing the value that comes from these relationships, most are still using these channels as a form of broadcast advertising. It's almost as if businesses have become anesthetized because of their reliance in the past on using media channels as a gateway to the consumer.

In the pre-Internet media world, your business could not have a direct relationship with the consumer. If you wanted to let people in your city know about your products or services, you had to take out advertising (few were great at direct marketing). The value of traditional media was not in the high quality of content that they produced, but rather in the direct relationship they had with an audience because of the perceived value of the content to the consumer. Now, in this world where consumers are liking, friending, tweeting, and +1-ing brands, not only have the tables turned, but the game has completely changed. And yet, if you look at what the majority of brands are doing in these digital spheres, you will be stunned:

- They're asking consumers to "like" them on Facebook while few actually make an effort to connect to those individuals on their own spaces. Here's a hint: Instead of asking people to like your business, why doesn't your business start liking these people first?
- They're asking customers to subscribe to the RSS feeds of their blogs or share their content, while the brand editors spend zero time engaging in the comments on the blogs being created by their customers. Here's a hint: Be active on every blog that serves your industry. Don't expect everyone to come to you.
- They're looking for customers to follow them on Twitter, but don't actually push beyond their own tweetstream to build affinity and loyalty. Here's a hint: If your Twitter feed is nothing but announcements about your sales or service

upgrades and nobody is retweeting or sharing your content, it may be time to start thinking about adapting your content strategy (more on that in chapter 9).

- They're asking customers to watch their videos on YouTube, but few brands are doing anything unique on this channel. It's mostly their traditional advertising or longer versions of TV ads. Hint: The Web isn't a receptacle for your TV ads and corporate videos. Get creative! You can show real demos, answer real questions, and give customers a sneak peek into what you're planning. What's better: begging for views or having people willfully share your content?

CREATE A NEW SCENARIO...

Many businesses create personas. These personas are fictional people who represent the "typical" customer. Most businesses have multiple personas because it's hard to pigeonhole people. These personas wind up being deep-dives into not only who these people are (demographics and psychographics), but also how they buy. The problem with the majority of the "how they buy" scenarios attached to these personas is that they have traditionally been very linear.

Here's some new "fiction" for you: Sophie needs a new pair of sunglasses. She goes online and does some research. She posts some options up on Facebook and asks her friends on Twitter and Pinterest to check them out and help her decide. Then she heads down to the store (if she hasn't already made the purchase online) to buy the sunglasses. Sounds realistic and simple enough, doesn't it? It's only half of the story.

Let's try that story again. Here's some nonfiction for you: Sophie needs a new pair of sunglasses. She does some online research (reads some peer-based reviews), posts some options on Facebook and Pinterest, and tweets them up. Her friend Rachel sees the tweet, and they text each other about heading over to the mall together. While strolling through the mall, not only are they both chatting to each other, but they're connected. They're responding to text messages, they're being alerted to Facebook and Twitter updates, they're laughing at posts, and—maybe—they're even checking in with foursquare (or some other location-based online social network) to see who else is around to join the outing (OMG, Lianna is already here at the mall!). While in the store, they notice a couple of other glasses, they snap some pictures and post them, but then a question comes up about the materials that were used to make the glasses. Sophie and Rachel do some quick online searches... nothing. They realize that the brand is on Twitter so they ask the brand directly... and so the story goes.

The new consumers are not linear. They are scattered. They are squiggly. They are connected—not only to one another, but also to the world—and their connectivity and engagement are highly untethered. I'm often critical of brands that try to make digital media bend to their will instead of spending the time, making the effort, and having the patience to build valuable credibility (which leads to loyalty and true direct relationships with the consumer).

Consumers are social... much more social than they have ever been before. If you think your consumers are (still) not social, that's going to change as well (quickly). These are not linear relationships (like the ones they've probably had with your flyers or coupons), and you're not going to be able to make them bend to your will either. The brands that build a better direct relationship with their consumers will be able to transcend the other challenges issued above. The opportunity is in recognizing that—finally—your business can reboot its relationship with your consumers like never before.

THIS IS NOT MY CUSTOMER.

Many businesses feel that technology (smartphones, iPads, and social media) has had no direct impact on them, because the tech-savvy consumer is not in their "demographic." This is the typical battle cry of those working in the B2B (business-to-business) sector. Nothing could be further from the truth. Relationships are at the very core of every business, and those with the strongest (and, yes, most direct) relationships win. The people who lament this massive shift in consumerism are, typically, the same group who used to wonder why they would ever need a website. Whether or not social media is a current part of your customers' media and technology diet is irrelevant, because it will be soon. The question is: How soon? Without the gift of crystal balls, you can still ask if it will be ten years? Five years? Two years?

My gut (which is driven by close to two decades of professional experience) says less than five years and actually closer to two years. If your brand is already in the planning process for next year, this means the topic needs to get on your business agenda now. Today. This new generation of direct relationships changes everything from how you answer your phones... to how you provide post-sale engagement... to how you speak, respond, and communicate in the business world. Direct relationships are no longer relegated to the social media channels, they're the way brands behave: online, offline, and otherwise.

GET A KICK IN THE PANTS FROM CHE-WEI WANG AND TAYLOR LEVY.

CW&T is a self-described "teeny design studio in Brooklyn" that is basically a two-person operation—designers Che-Wei Wang and Taylor Levy. I have a certain kinship with these two because we all love the Pilot Hi-Tec-C pen, which unfortunately isn't readily available in North America. The .25 mm fine tip writes like a dream (better than most Montblancs out there, by my estimation), but it looks and feels like your average (read: cheap) ballpoint pens. As designers, Che-Wei and Levy set out to design a simple, classy, and indestructible pen that could house the 0.3 mm black Hi-Tec-C cartridge. What they came up with was something they dubbed Pen Type-A. Without knowing if there would be a market for Pen Type-A and not having the resources to turn this design concept into any semblance of a serious business model, they turned to one of the hottest online destinations, Kickstarter, to get a feel for the potential market.

If you don't know about Kickstarter, well, now's the time for you to find out: Kickstarter is a simple crowdfunding platform that allows individuals to post their creative projects (everything from music and film to technology and journalism) and to start an online threshold-pledge system for the funding of the project. It is, without question, the most interesting thing happening online right now.

In short: If you can't get a movie deal, you can post your project to Kickstarter, define the budget, and invite anybody and everybody who thinks it's a good idea to become a backer. This doesn't mean that a backer is an investor in the actual company; rather, backers are pre-paying for a product that has yet to be developed (creators establish different levels for backing a project and what those levels receive in terms of products and services).

This is a massive shift in what it means to be an entrepreneur or entrepreneurial. In the past, the largest hurdle to moving from business ideation to execution was the chasm of question marks in between those two worlds. Many people have great ideas that can be explained in simple three-minute online videos, but very few people have the skills to then execute the ideas successfully.

Kickstarter has reduced the mountain between ideation and execution into the proverbial molehill. Now, by posting their ideas with a clear financial structure on Kickstarter, businesses can find out—in short order—if there really is a market for their wares.

Kickstarter is a New York startup that was founded in April 2009. According to Wikipedia, the company has raised more than $275 million for more than sixty-five thousand projects since it got started. Even more impressive, Kickstarter has a project success rate of close to 45 percent. (Success is defined by whether the project met or surpassed the threshold set by the project organizers or creators.) The company makes its money by taking a percentage of the funded projects. It serves as an amazing place to see business, creativity, and entrepreneurship come together, but it also acts as a beacon shining on the power of direct relationships.

What better way is there to know whether there is a market for your business idea than by putting that idea "out there" and enabling those who take an interest in it to put their money where their mouths are? These backers are paying customers—they just happen to be paying for something long before it is ever produced. They are the spirit and embodiment of a direct relationship. In 2004, Chris Anderson (the former editor in chief at *Wired* magazine) wrote the bestselling business book *The Long Tail*. The book describes a new economy that has emerged online because we are no longer limited by the physical retail store space and how much inventory can be sold per square foot. Because of online commerce, it now makes sense for companies to sell products that would have been purchased by only a handful of people, because they can make serious money selling these more obscure items online instead of only selling a limited number of more popular items. They do this because of the new power we find in direct relationships.

Apple co-founder Steve Jobs was known for saying that it's

not the customers' job to know what they want. There's also that old Henry Ford saying, "If I had asked people what they wanted, they would have said faster horses" (although the *Harvard Business Review* recently published an article claiming that there is no evidence Ford ever said that). Regardless, we tend to think that the true business leaders are the ones who can see into the future. The ones who recognize a new market where there isn't one. If that's the case, it also explains why there aren't that many truly revolutionary business leaders: The risk is huge, and having a true vision for a product or service that doesn't exist can be a solitary place to be . . . until now.

DIRECT RELATIONSHIPS MINIMIZE RISK.

Kickstarter does more than initiate interesting and obscure projects; it helps kick-start businesses by matching them with consumers who are interested in a direct relationship.

The platform doesn't begin and end with a project being funded. The entire journey is often shared (both on Kickstarter and other online social networking channels), so that the relationship between the consumers (the backers) and the creators can strengthen through the process. With Kickstarter, business owners can figure out if they're producing something that people actually want, instead of producing something and then having to create the market for it.

At first blush, Kickstarter seems foreign given how we have seen business to date, but doing some digging into it reveals that it may be the smartest way for businesses to develop true direct relationships with consumers: by getting them involved in defining the value of the products long before they go into production.

Remember the Pen Type-A project? Wang and Levy set a threshold of $2,500. On August 15, 2011, they surpassed their threshold to the tune of $281,989, from more than four thousand backers. That sounds like a solid first year of sales considering the product doesn't even exist yet—not to mention the four thousand strong and loyal direct relationships that have been created.

Is this all new media hyperbole? Does this truly have an effect on business? Consider this last piece of data from the Kickstarter world: In February 2012, Yancey Strickler (one of Kickstarter's co-founders) said in an interview with *Talking Points Memo* that Kickstarter was on course to disburse over $150 million to its various projects in 2012. To put this into perspective, the National Endowment for the Arts had a fiscal 2012 budget of $146 million. On top of that, several Kickstarter projects have topped $1 million in funding from backers. As Kickstarter's popularity continues to grow and inspires new and exciting entrepreneurs, we're starting to see that businesses that create powerful direct relationships based on value can achieve staggering financial results.

If you had a dream to manufacture a watch, where would you turn? In a world where more and more people use their smartphones as their timepieces, watches are increasingly transitioning from an essential utility to a non-required stylish accessory. Could a new kind of wristwatch even be worth the effort to develop and find a marketplace? Pebble Technology out of Palo Alto had a crazy dream to design and manufacture a new kind of watch that would be driven by technology. They wanted the face of the watch to use e-ink technology (the same type of high-resolution screen that you would find on an Amazon Kindle e-reader) coupled with touch technology (so that users can receive text messages, use caller ID, get emails, and control other electronic devices by touching and swiping the watch's faceplate like an iPad). They posted their dream and a working prototype of the Pebble e-paper watch for iPhone and Android last year. They were looking to secure $100,000 as a "feeler" to quantify public interest in this type of smartwatch. Much to their surprise, a staggering $10,266,845 worth of watches was sold in a matter of weeks.

Not only was their business model almost instantly validated, but the power of direct relationships pushed demand for their product well beyond their means. It was a veritable "sellout," and as Pebble Technology scrambled to hire enough people and find the right suppliers to turn this watch from a video into a real-world product, they kept their direct relationships alive with constant updates on both the Kickstarter page and in their own social spaces. Their future consumers became active participants (evangelists and cheerleaders) for Pebble Technology—right down to choosing colors for the wristband.

CAN YOU CREATE A DOMINO EFFECT LIKE THAT WITH YOUR BUSINESS?

When news broke in late 2010 that famed business thinker and bestselling business book author Seth Godin (*Linchpin*, *Tribes*, *Purple Cow*, *All Marketers Are Liars*, etc.) was going to stop publishing books "traditionally," every armchair business quarterback had an opinion. The news hit Twitter like a fake celebrity death scandal (especially among marketing nerds, like yours truly). In actuality, Godin wound up launching his own publishing company, called The Domino Project (a yearlong endeavor), in partnership with Amazon in 2011. While some publishers took his yearlong plan to mean that the business was not viable, Godin took to his highly trafficked blog to explain that "it was a project, not a lifelong commitment to being a publisher of books. Projects are fun to start, but part of the deal is that they don't last forever. The goal was to explore what could be done in a fast-changing environment."

In this reboot environment, Godin managed to publish twelve books (all of which became bestsellers on Amazon), only two of which (*Poke the Box* and *We Are All Weird*) were authored by Godin. Once he finished his "experiment," Godin then took to Kickstarter for the launch of another book titled *The Icarus Deception*. Within a handful of hours, this project hit its goal of $40,000 and then went on to secure more than $250,000 in funding from his readers and fans. The lesson from The Domino Project and *The Icarus Deception* is less about how long it lasted or how many books they cumulatively sold, and more about what it means to nurture and build a world of direct relationships. In the end, The Domino Project and *The Icarus Deception* have been put in front of over one million readers. And that was the whole point: to pinpoint fans and followers and to keep connecting to them.

THIS IS THE FUTURE OF BUSINESS THINKING.

So can you (or your business) be like Seth Godin? The answer is "maybe." We tend to see one act: "Seth leaves major book publishing behind." What we forget is the track record (twelve bestselling business books, as many speaking events per year as he would like to do, his own seminars, thousands of blog posts, free ebooks, and more goodwill than you can shake a tweet at). This amounts to decades of doing tons of things (let's not forget about his Web destination, Squidoo, that allows anybody to create a quick webpage) that all gave him direct connections with the people who will buy his books from him, talk about him to their peers, and evangelize his thinking. Godin built up his direct relationships with his readers and fans over the span of nearly two decades.

Remember, direct relationships don't happen overnight. They

come only from a concerted effort—by the entire business—to make them an engine of business growth that everyone is not only taking part in, but also accountable for.

Can you really say that you have this kind of relationship with your consumers? What Godin, the *Wall Street Journal*, the book publishing industry, and literary agents aren't telling you is that you can, in fact, be just like Seth Godin. These new and powerful digital channels are here for you (and they're free—if you don't count the time and effort you need to put into them). In text, images, audio, and video, you too can publish how you think to the world...instantly. You too can share with others, build direct relationships, and get your ideas to spread. You do not have to rely solely on mass media as a gatekeeper to spread the word. And you'll know in short order if your ideas have traction. On top of that, you'll be able to track how an idea spreads and connects (more on that in the next chapter). In the end, you (and your business) are not Seth Godin, but you can be.

LESSONS ABOUT BUILDING DIRECT RELATIONSHIPS...

Now comes the hard work of taking all of this information and crystallizing it in relation to the work that you do. *There is no linear "how-to" on building direct relationships.* What works for one company will not work for another, and the successes that we have seen in this chapter aren't indicative of future success based on a specific industry or type of consumer that you are chasing. The following chapters will help illuminate opportunities to get you closer to your consumers in this world where they are all connected. That all being said, there are some consistent philosophies that we can pull out and begin to execute. Here are five of them, which serve as a primer for creating valuable direct relationships:

Lesson #1—Deliver value first.

If the expectation is that someone will follow or like you and all you give in return are self-serving contests and promotions to drive awareness, not only are you interrupting (and annoying) people, but you're completely missing the bigger opportunity. *Provide value first.* Not just on pricing and service, but in the information that you provide. Famed sales author Jeffrey Gitomer (*The Sales Bible, Little Red Book of Selling, Social BOOM!*, and so on . . .) told an audience of mortgage providers that the easiest way to close a sale is to say the following to the prospect: "I'm going to find you the best and most affordable mortgage, even if that means not buying it from me." Would you give that person your business? Your loyalty? That mortgage provider is doing one simple thing: giving value first.

Lesson #2—Be open.

If your business is based on secrets and black boxes, consumers will have an underlying feeling of resentment. The digital world has changed the business rules. It's hard to keep quiet about bad service in a hotel when there are websites like TripAdvisor. You need a culture of openness and transparency. This doesn't mean divulging your secret sauce recipe; it simply means that you can never engender the spirit of building a direct relationship when the core business function is to the pull the wool over someone else's eyes.

Lesson #3—Be clear and consistent.

The majority of brands these days deploy a "spray and pray" mentality toward how they connect to their consumers. They wait for moments in time or a specific time of the year. Parlay that thinking to the relationship you have with your spouse: Would that same model work? The best relationships are the ones in which communication is both clear and consistent.

The best relationships develop slowly over time and are nurtured on a day-to-day basis. The important component of this is not to become too overbearing by not being sensitive to your customers' true needs. Fatigue is normal. After a certain amount of time, constant emails from a brand to a very loyal follower will cause fatigue. Understand and respond to this ebb and flow.

Lesson #4—Create a mutually beneficial world.

In the case of Beats By Dre and Target, it's not healthy to be going after each individual for the "like" on Facebook. The true opportunity is to figure out how to create a mutually beneficial world, instead of one where you are now competing with your own partners.

Lesson #5—True fans.

The majority of people do not want to friend or like your brand. They use their social graphs for friends, family, and those they made fun of in high school. The intrusion of brands is simply that: an intrusion. Your business will never get everyone to like it.

So instead, turn to the fanatical. Find and nurture your true fans. Your heavy users. As that relationship delivers, they will become evangelists for you and you will begin to experience the network effect.

IT'S NOT (PERFECTLY) CLEAR.

Look at everything from your business development and sales to your marketing and public relations. Is what you're doing based on nurturing a more direct and personal relationship with your consumers, or are you simply blasting corporate messaging out through the channels? This fostering of direct relationships is what will move you forward through purgatory. It will bring you from a place where you are positioning messages to a place where you are providing true utility to your consumers.

CHAPTER 2

Give Me Utility (Or Give Me Death)

The shift from broadcasting and pandering to utilitarianism marketing.

THE NEW *REAL ESTATE.*

What is the golden rule of the real estate business? Location, location, location. And for businesses, location is everything.

Whether it's a corporate head office or a massive retailer, where you put that physical entity has a direct correlation to your success. Here's a new spin on that theory: With people spending more and more of their time looking, reviewing, and shopping online, the *new* real estate is whatever screen is in front of the consumer.

How great does a brand have to be to earn a coveted place on the home screen of a consumer's iPhone? Recent data and research do not speak kindly to how well brands are integrating into these new neighborhoods and communities. In the *Digiday* news item "Saving Abandoned Brand Mobile Apps" (March 29, 2012), Giselle Abramovich reports that one in four mobile apps are never used again after being downloaded and that 26 percent of apps aren't used more than once. Do you think it is because these are *branded* apps? Probably not. The likely (and brutally honest) answer is this: Most branded apps suck.

THE NEW *NARCISSISM.*

Brands have to get over themselves. The majority of apps are failing because they add no value to the smartphone user. There is no utility. The apps are self-centered catalogs—nothing more than a showcase for products and services. There's a bigger picture and a bigger story here. If one in four branded apps aren't used again after being downloaded and 26 percent of branded apps aren't used more than once, I'm here to promise you that 100 percent of customers use, keep, and talk about the branded apps that provide true value to them and their lives.

Let me give you an example...

I GOTTA GO. NOW.

How often have you had that feeling in the pit of your stomach and suddenly it's tunnel vision... You have to go... Now. *You need a bathroom.*

I'll spare you the details of my sometimes-sensitive stomach scenarios, but as someone who travels over a hundred thousand miles every year, I can tell you that finding a clean bathroom is often a source of concern.

I'll do my best to wait until I'm in the comforts of my hotel room or make a lunge for the airport lounge, but if you ever find yourself in the middle of New York City and nature calls, what are you to do? Enter SitOrSquat.

Laugh all you want, but SitOrSquat resides on my iPhone's homepage. The app allows users to find clean bathrooms (along with changing tables, handicapped access, and other bathroom features) with ease. By knowing your phone's location, the app quickly shows you how close you are to a clean public restroom (and a map to get there). It's a wiki-like platform where the content and ratings are governed by us—the loyal users.

You can rate, comment, and even add the toilets of your choice. In March 2009, P&G's Charmin launched a global sponsorship of SitOrSquat—and by the looks of it, the toilet paper brand has backed a winner, because when most people talk about SitOr-Squat, they're also talking about Charmin. Charmin...a toilet paper company...is giving their consumers a true utility.

In short—and to me—this app is totally win-win.

BRANDS WILL NEED TO MAKE THEIR MARKETING MORE USEFUL. PERIOD. END OF SENTENCE.

It's a cluttered world. It's an even more cluttered marketing world. Brands still think it's all about the pomp and circumstance. It is...and it isn't. No one (especially me) is going to deny that a well-executed Super Bowl ad gets attention, gets a brand noticed, and results in lift (sales, brand awareness, whatever). No one is going to deny that a well-played experiential marketing event builds buzz and gets attention. There are many online media properties that have very convincing data to back up the purchase of a homepage takeover ad. Making noise can create noise in the marketplace. The challenge comes when you shift over to the newer digital marketing platforms. The tendency is to think like an advertiser. In this moment of purgatory, the answer is to think about providing utility.

It's obvious that just having a Facebook page, YouTube channel, Twitter feed, or whatever can get a brand to accumulate followers and friends at a fast-and-furious pace. Consumers like feeling that they're a part of an inner circle or among the first to know something. Brands are great at dangling those carrots in front of consumers who are willing to click a like or follow or +1 button.

But it can be a dangerous game of diminishing returns. All marketing initiatives face the reality of fatigue—it happens in direct marketing, it happens in email marketing, and it's going to happen in social media (it's already happening). People get tired (pretty quickly) of the same old, same old.

THE RISE OF UTILITARIANISM MARKETING.

Utilitarianism marketing is going to be the next great business disrupter.

What is utilitarianism marketing? It's not about advertising, it's not about messaging, and it's not about immediate conversions. It's about providing a true value and utility: something consumers not only would want to use—constantly and consistently—but would derive so much value from it that it would be given front-and-center attention in their lives. Do you think your brand has the ability to create that kind of interest and attention in this media-saturated and ads-everywhere world in which we live?

When something out of the marketing department doesn't have a huge splash around it or a billboard in Times Square for the senior management team to point at, it tends to get yawns. The yawns happen because the numbers don't look the same when benchmarked against traditional mass media or other forms of advertising. Actually giving consumers something valuable seems counterintuitive to most marketing departments because they equate "value" with "cost," and the last thing a marketer wants to do is give something that costs them more money to fewer people than they are reaching with their traditional advertising. The truth is that great utilitarianism marketing doesn't have to cost more. *It just has to be useful.*

Last year, I was in a business meeting when the idea for an iPhone app came up. It was a smart idea (you know, the kind of idea that you wish you had thought of). The chief marketing officer smiled during the presentation, put his hand up to ask a question, removed the glasses from his eyes and placed them on his notebook, folded his hands, leaned forward, and said, "It's genius...but can we put our four key brand messages in there as well, because if we don't force people to look at them, what's the point of this app?"

IF YOU GIVE SOMETHING TO PEOPLE THAT THEY ACTUALLY WANT AND NEED...THEY WILL LOVE YOU FOREVER.

It seems simple enough, doesn't it? Something that is useful to a consumer...truly useful, without a sales pitch, without in-your-face marketing messaging...is the next generation of marketing. People are smart. They'll figure it out. They'll think, *I can't live without this app...I can't believe Brand X just gave it to me...how cool is that?*

SO IF A TOILET PAPER COMPANY HAS FIGURED IT OUT, WHAT'S GOT YOU ALL BLOCKED UP?

These are the early days of utilitarianism marketing. We know this to be true because the majority of the funds that are allocated to initiatives like this tend to come out of the marketing department's experimental budget. *Experimental* is code for "We'll try it, and if it works we'll act like we always knew that it would because we're geniuses...but if it fails we can just label it an experiment and no one will lose their job."

How long do you think that line of thinking will last?

The benefit of finding ourselves in this moment of purgatory is that we are confronted with open fields: vast white spaces there for us to spend the time to figure out what consumers want and how to own that very precious commodity of real estate also known as the screen in front of them.

OWNING THE COMPLETE EXPERIENCE.

Nike is one of those iconic brands that is hard to replicate. The lesson from their massive success is that it takes a unique perspective and approach to break through—especially if your business is something as generic as sports shoes and apparel. Over the years, the company has been innovative in everything from product development (pouring liquid rubber on a waffle iron to get a better tread for a running shoe...really?) to coming up with culture-changing advertising campaigns ("Just Do It") that not only advanced the company's target market, but inspired non-sports-interested people to get up off the couch, put down the remote and potato chips, and start moving. When you think about it, these are profoundly powerful movements. The push of "Just Do It" spoke to every man, woman, and child. It was a battle cry for more people to think more seriously about their health and well-being.

By creating this awakening, Nike also created many, many more customers. If people suddenly bought into this advertising slogan and decided to take a jog instead of watching another episode of *Storage Wars*, they needed some basic workout gear. There have been multiple brand and marketing extensions from these innovations (from new breakthroughs in running shoes

to advertising campaigns targeted specifically at empower-
ing women)—and let's not forget the other massive movements
that Nike has created and nurtured, like the Lance Armstrong
Livestrong yellow bracelet campaign (prior to the scandal), Nike+
for those who want to meet and sync their running with their
smartphones and their online social networks, and many other
innovative experiential events. Nike does a fantastic job of leveraging the power of broadcast advertising while constantly creating true utility for customers.

So what kind of a company is Nike? Would you be surprised to
hear one media journalist define them as a technology company?

The annual South by Southwest conference (known as SXSW)
has changed dramatically since its humble beginnings as a little-
known Austin, Texas, music festival in 1987. Over the years,
SXSW has evolved beyond just music into film and interactive.
The interactive component of the festival has grown by leaps
and bounds; this is now the preeminent conference where new
ideas and technologies are discovered. Over the years, many have
pointed to SXSW for helping to tip companies like Twitter and
foursquare over the point. With each successive year, the buzz
building up to the conference filters down to one question: What
will be the latest bright and shiny object that we'll all be playing with after this year's SXSW? Would it surprise you that the
answer for the 2012 conference was . . . the FuelBand by Nike?

Digiday's Jack Marshall, reporting from the 2012 edition of
SXSW, could hardly contain himself when he published the article "Why Nike Is a Tech Company" (March 12, 2012). It turns out
that the breakthrough technology at last year's SXSW was Nike's
launch and promotion of FuelBand.

FuelBand is a very cool-looking lighted bracelet that measures
your physical activity and awards you with Fuel (aka points). The

more you move, the more fuel you are awarded (yes, Nike has figured out a way to add gamification to your daily routine). You set the amount of Fuel per day that you would ideally like to achieve, and the bracelet will notify you as to how you're doing. It ties in with a mobile app that lets you compare and contrast your goals with others' performances. What Nike+ did for runners, Fuel-Band can do for the rest of us.

FuelBand is just another product that Nike has produced for a line they now call Digital Sport. Nike is establishing itself not only as a technology company, but also as a benchmark case study in what it takes to shift from an advertising-driven marketing organization into one that is all about utility...and making money from that utility as well.

Joseph Jaffe (author of *Life After the 30-Second Spot*, *Join the Conversation*, and *Flip the Funnel*) waited nearly an hour in line at the SXSW pop-up retail experience that Nike built to launch FuelBand to the world's digital tastemakers. After a "fitting" session with one of their sales reps, Jaffe found himself walking back to his hotel room when he suddenly realized that he had not even looked at how much the FuelBand had cost. The $140 wristband has become much more than a topic of conversation when people see it blink and blip on Jaffe's wrist—in fact, it has helped him shed over twenty pounds (and still shedding). Jaffe also admits that the wristband is a constant reminder of Nike and that he not only is fine with it, but appreciates their help in his battle against the bulge.

The lesson Nike is teaching the rest of us is that when your brand can provide that kind of deep utility, people will not only want more from it, but they will take their connectedness to the brand to a whole other plane of existence, passion, and care. In short, another win-win, where the brand is not only providing utility but making serious money doing it.

AUGMENTING REALITY ADDS ANOTHER BRICK TO UTILITY.

When I was a kid, I was a massive fan of LEGO (I still am). Think back to those childhood days. Your parents would take you to the department store, you would stand in front of what seemed like a Mount Everest filled with every type of LEGO imaginable, and you would dream about all the cool things you could build. How often did you find yourself grabbing a box and wondering if the contents would be too complex for you? The technique many of us deployed at that time was to pick up the box, place it next to our ear, and shake it—as if the sound of LEGOs smacking against one another inside a closed box could provide any level of comfort or information as to the level of skill it would require to assemble.

Well, you can stop all that shaking now. LEGO not only sells their sets through mass retailers but in 2010 the company started opening up their own branded stores to answer the call of box shakers the world over.

With close to fifty stores globally, LEGO needed a reason to convince people who would normally go to a toy store, big-box retailer, or department store to instead pay a visit to a store that only sells LEGO. In every LEGO store, you will now find what looks like a standard kiosk. It is not standard—by any stretch of the imagination. At what's known as the LEGO Digital Box, customers can choose any LEGO box in the store; when they stand in front of the Digital Box, the screen on the kiosk is able to recognize the exact product, and then create a three-dimensional rendering of what is in the box (this technology is known as augmented reality, which can best be described as using a screen and an Internet connection to add a layer of information or visualization on top of what you are looking at).

The Digital Box kiosk actually builds the contents of the LEGO box virtually on screen, so that you can see both size and scale of complexity. You can move the box around and see every angle of what the construction toy will look like once it is fully built. It even adds animation, so you'll see the tiny LEGO people running around, the propellers on the planes spinning, and more. It's much more than an in-store experience, it's a functional utility that allows both kids and parents to see what, exactly, they're actually buying.

IT DOESN'T HAVE TO BE SEXY. IT HAS TO BE USEFUL.

Nike, LEGO, and Procter & Gamble. Understandably, they have budgets that you probably can't compete with, and they're able to try things that most brands can only dream of. But you don't need unlimited budgets to make your app work in a big way.

Example: The Nationwide Mobile App (yes, the insurance company) is for people who've just been in a car accident. It's a useful step-by-step application that walks consumers through everything from collecting and exchanging accident information to taking pictures of the accident scene and recording the location (using the iPhone's built-in GPS capabilities); it even has a flashlight in case the accident happens at night. It's not an ad. It's not push marketing. It's utilitarianism marketing. It also does away with those handwritten accident reports that are usually so poorly done because everyone's hands are shaking from having just been in an accident.

This clever app was pushed into the iPhone app store in 2009 and does a lot more than document an accident with multimedia. If you have ever had to deal with an insurance company, you know how long, hard, and arduous the claim process can be. Just hop online and do some generic searches; you'll uncover thousands of complaints from people who are spending hours on the phone and writing letters to get a claim settled.

While I'm sure that, like many of their competitors, Nationwide has its challenges, their on-scene accident app clearly helps expedite claims. Along with the car accident report tools, the Nationwide mobile app allows customers to start their claims right away. Customers can even let Nationwide know the best times for representatives to connect with them for follow-ups, and it includes lists of Nationwide Blue Ribbon Repair Services Facilities and local towing services. Nationwide's ability to deliver on a utilitarianism marketing initiative allows them to understand the pain points of the customer and to not only alleviate that pain, but also create a better customer experience. The customer utility that Nationwide Mobile App delivers is something the company could have never offered before. Another win-win.

LESSONS FROM UTILITARIANISM MARKETING...

Lesson #1—It's not you, it's me.

As you begin thinking about creating utilitarianism marketing extensions for your own brand, stop thinking about what you would like your customers to do (buy more of your stuff, see more of your products, come to your store more often, or refer more people to you).

When you do utilitarianism marketing well, those outcomes become the natural effect, but they are not the primary driver. Always remember this: Make it about your customers' needs. A great utility is something that adds tremendous value to individuals' lives—and in doing so, makes them more naturally aligned with your brand. It's not about you . . . it's about them.

Think about it this way: Utility first, brand second (a very, very distant second).

Lesson #2—Remove friction.

All the examples given in this chapter have one common (if not subtle) attribute: They remove a point of friction. LEGO is able to show you the simplicity (or complexity) of what is in the box. Nationwide makes a moment of shock and fear less stressful by providing you with the tools to capture every aspect of a car accident while your head may be in another space. Nike is able to provide you with both a reminder and a record of just how active you are. Each of these brands is removing a source of consumer friction.

For you to be successful, you will have to spend a lot more time acting like one of your customers instead of sitting behind a desk trying to get them to buy. When your form of utilitarianism marketing can remove the friction, you will have a winner.

Lesson #3—No expectations.

Create it, give it out, and spread it with no expectations.

Now, this is going to be a tough pill for you and your business to swallow. This may even be the showstopper in terms of getting the funding and buy-in to bring it to market, but don't let this lesson point stop you.

If it truly is a source of utility—something you and everybody you know will use—then push forward. It will work. Just imagine being in that first marketing meeting for Charmin at P&G when someone came up with the idea of partnering with SitOr-Squat. Someone there presented the concept well, and the brass bought in. You too should go into your presentation in the spirit of no expectations, but knowing that the value is there. If, after monitoring the situation, you're not seeing the uptake or adoption, take a close look and make a sound business call on it.

I'm sure Charmin didn't expect SitOrSquat to outperform their television commercial buys. But I am sure they knew that the utility of SitOrSquat would not only get them media attention, but enable them to connect the brand to consumers in ways that a thirty-second TV spot never could.

Lesson #4—The ultimate question.

Do you know what the ultimate question for your business is?

The evolution of customer service and brand loyalty is a topic that has captured the imagination of Fred Reichheld for over twenty years. In 1996, the Bain fellow published his first book, *The Loyalty Effect: The Hidden Force Behind Growth, Profits, and Lasting Value.* Two years ago, Reichheld (along with co-author Rob Markey) published a newly updated version of his seminal 2006 book, *The Ultimate Question* (now titled *The Ultimate Question 2.0*).

Reichheld was looking to uncover one simple question that businesses of any size, serving any industry, could ask customers to figure out if they were loyal and would buy from them again. The ultimate question—as defined by Reichheld—is this: "How likely is it that you would recommend this company to a friend or colleague?" A business's ability to not only understand the answer to this question but also benchmark their success led Reichheld to create and champion the Net Promoter Score system—which companies the world over now use to define how much love their consumers actually have for them. The core value that Reichheld is hoping businesses use to benchmark their success is just as relevant—if not more so—when looking at utilitarianism marketing. That is, think about what you would like to create and ask yourself the ultimate question—just replace the word *company* with your marketing initiative. Pushing that concept just a little bit further, be insanely honest with yourself as well and ask, "Would I put this on the homepage of my iPhone?"

If you would not, keep working until you uncover a utility that would reside in that most highly precious piece of digital real estate.

Lesson #5—KISS.

KISS stands, of course, for "Keep It Simple, Stupid."

I've been in brainstorming meetings and seen an original idea pushed in so many different directions that the resulting initiative gets too big and too complex. There are simple tricks that we often dismiss because we think that technology has all of the answers. If a car company wants one thousand people to take their car out for a test drive, instead of building a very complex social media platform, why not simply print up some business cards with an offer to test-drive it and put them on the windshields of cars in shopping malls where you think people may be willing to go for it? (But please, don't break any laws by doing it!)

No, I'm not saying that you should dismiss modern technology and all the amazing ways that we can now share and find information and tools. I *am* saying that you need to explore everything . . . even the options that, initially, seem too simple to work. One of the best parts of that Nationwide Mobile app is the flashlight. Flashlight apps are nothing new on the iPhone, but it was the simple, kind thought of the developers of that app to include a flashlight that makes it so holistically powerful.

When you start thinking about utility, there is no need to boil the ocean. Consider not only how to keep it simple, but how to make it do one thing (maybe two things) great. LEGO's Digital Box lets you do just one thing: see what's inside the box. Keep it simple.

Lesson #6—Make it now.

We lead very busy and complex lives. We're inundated with brands and messaging at every turn. No place is safe. Even our smartphones are quickly becoming our own mini versions of Times Square hell, and it's very hard to fight.

True utility happens in the moment of need. Not the brand's moment of need, but the *consumer's* moment of need. If you can meet that need when the customer needs it met, you are on to something big.

Example: Skullcandy is a very hip audio headphone company (though they have expanded into other related areas). They offer loud patterns and a fresh look for a customer who's tired of the standard choice between white and black headphones. Like many brands, Skullcandy is doing its best to rise above being a basic consumer electronics goods company, and is now close to becoming a lifestyle brand. Their mobile app (which features functionality including streaming music and video, and has content related to customers' lifestyles) delivers geo-located destinations for surf, skate, snow, and motocross, along with up-to-the-second weather reports. So not only can you find that brand-new and just-listed dirt bike trail that someone else discovered, you can also see what the wind is like at the beach (in case you would like to go surfing instead). That's the type of utility that Skullcandy consumers need right now...in the moment.

Lesson #7—Ride on the backs of giants.

Always remember, you're not necessarily looking to invent the next iPad (but if you've got it, run with it).

However, you should be looking to take advantage of everything that the iPad has brought with it and then make it work for you. Look for pockets (very, very small pockets) of innovation that can work within the framework of something already established.

The ideal way to get started is to look at what people are very excited about today. Can your brand fit within something that is new and exciting based on what the new iPhone has to offer? Is there something that you can do with Pinterest or Instagram or Facebook? These are established giants, and there's nothing wrong with figuring out a point of utility that adds value to those channels while providing your consumers with a whole new level of service.

HootSuite has been doing a great job of riding on the backs of giants. Founded in 2008, the company set out to answer a simple question: Is there a better way to use Twitter? Twitter provides users with a very linear experience. On any given screen, you are simply able to see a river of tweets in chronological order. Could there be a way to see a whole lot more of what's happening on Twitter three-dimensionally?

As more and more people are talking, interacting, and discussing brands, people, and whatever is on their mind, the traditional Twitter interface has revealed severe limitations. If you want to do any kind of formal search for keywords or hashtags on Twitter, you have to use the Twitter search functionality. If you want to create a shortened URL link, you have to find one of the many resources (like TinyURL or bitly). If you want to see more than one conversation on Twitter, it used to be there were no options...until brands like HootSuite arrived (there are now competitors like TweetDeck and others).

Simply put, HootSuite turns Twitter into a three-dimensional experience. It's a social media management system that not only makes Twitter a better user experience, but also integrates Facebook, LinkedIn, Google+, tumblr, and many more social media experiences into one cohesive place. With the ability to view multiple columns (and multiple accounts) at once, you can see everything that is going on in your social media world (and even filter out the content that you do not want to see). Their browser-based software allows a team of people within a company to better manage the entire social media ecosystem.

HootSuite is both robust and addictive. Depending on how you customize it (and there's plenty of customizing to be done), you can create a full-on nerve center for your brand, products, services, and competitors. As of January 2012, HootSuite had over three million users with more than seven hundred million messages sent. By riding on the backs of giants such as Twitter, Facebook, Google, and more, the company has raised millions of dollars in venture capital investment with an estimated valuation of $500 million.

Ride on the backs of giants, just like HootSuite has done.

WHY DON'T MORE BRANDS MAKE THEMSELVES MORE USEFUL?

We could very well see a day soon when utilitarianism marketing budgets overshadow those of broadcast advertising.

Look no further than the massive growth of content marketing (more on that in chapter 9). Content marketing's core function is to provide true value to a consumer that will trigger an inbound marketing effect (where the consumer comes to you instead of you broadcasting a message you hope people will see). The programming and development of mobile apps are becoming both simpler and cheaper to do (in much the same way that WordPress and tumblr democratized the ability to create and publish blogs and websites). These changes are only going to happen much faster as the technology evolves.

In the current marketplace, the opportunity to capitalize on utilitarianism marketing is wide open. And once you provide true value, consumers will see no reason to even look at your competitors. Within our current state of purgatory lie countless opportunities for businesses to rise above. Understanding the new consumer is critical for your ability to not only provide a new level of utility but to make it through purgatory.

CHAPTER 3

Built to Touch

The convergence of passive and active media.

WELCOME TO MEDIA PURGATORY.

Do you love your job? Do you love the work that you're doing?

Look at the raw data: Most people are not all that happy. The majority of folks in the Western world work hard all day at a job they don't love, so when they come home they just want to sit down, relax, sip a beer, and let the television wash over them. They don't want to think about the day they just had, and they definitely don't want to think about the day that is coming tomorrow.

Media has traditionally been there to help people forget about all of that. Media has anesthetized us to reality for decades. The fundamental success of media platforms—like television—is driven by the fact that they are passive consumer experiences. You don't have to do much when you're in front of a TV—and that includes thinking.

Before the rise of social media, consumers mostly consumed the media (like reading a newspaper or listening to the radio). Now you see many major media companies asking consumers to chat, share, friend, like, link, and tweet. For over a decade, the word most often bandied about within major media corporations' boardrooms was *convergence*. Now what? Do we really expect the TV to be like the Internet? Can a newspaper simply go digital and regain its media prominence? Do passive consumers suddenly wake up and get active with all this media? These are important questions for you to think about when it comes to your business. Your ability to communicate and market your goods and services is suddenly in a state of media purgatory.

THE SHIFT TO TV EVERYWHERE.

We have to remember that our relationship with television has always been based on two pillars:

1. **Destination.** From "Must See TV" to your favorite sitcoms on Thursday night, you could always tell what the conversation around the watercooler was going to be about the next day at the office based on the schedule in *TV Guide*. We did things (like get home from work and eat supper) at specific times so as not to miss our favorite shows, and we shared in a collective moment—shared with everyone else watching—in the privacy of our homes.

    TV was never everywhere. It was always *only* in our living rooms and basements (it slowly crept into our bedrooms as well). This is changing rapidly. The captive audience was once a key component for advertising: Everyone was just sitting there, so messages would be right in front of them.

2. **Passivity.** Media can be both passive and active. Clearly, the Internet is an active media. Facebook is no fun at all if all you do is creep through your friend's pictures. We create, collaborate, share, friend, like, follow, and express ourselves. Even with all the interactivity that has recently been introduced,

however, most of us still enjoy TV passively. It's nice to shut the lid on the MacBook Air, sit back on the couch, and watch some Charlie Rose. TV was always passive entertainment. But as we have all seen, that is rapidly changing as well. People are increasingly more interested in sharing and chatting online *while* they're watching certain TV shows at specific times.

As human beings have become increasingly untethered (we are always connected through our smartphones and tablets), so too has television. With smartphones and iPads now promoting content—where, when, and how we consumers want it—this trend is not being lost on television. According to the MediaPost news item "ABC Studies iPad: Redefines TV Viewing" (October 7, 2011), "The iPad surely will play a role in accentuating that lesser connection to time and place going forward." The news item goes on to identify three emerging TV viewing trends that are new to our world:

1. **Micro-mobility.** Consumers would like TV content *on demand*, but not just from the comforts of their homes. Now they want it everywhere—from the beach and on their commutes to work to their backyards—and across multiple devices.
2. **Parallel play.** Your wife is watching *American Pickers* on television while you're sitting next to her watching an episode of *Diners, Drive-Ins and Dives* on your iPad. Parallel play is when two people are in the same room but watching different shows on different platforms and devices.
3. **Marathoning.** If it weren't for marathoning, I would have never been able to see *Mad Men* or *Breaking Bad*. Marathoning is when a viewer watches multiple episodes of the same show, one after the other. This trend has become so massive

that certain specialty and cable channels run their own marathons of their own shows.

WHERE IS THE MONEY?

The promise to television, radio, and newspaper advertisers was all about having a captive audience at a set time on a set date. The eyeballs of consumers were everything. Yes, branding power has now been extended because people routinely use a DVR or download their shows from iTunes. But this changes the advertising model (and how advertising is both consumed, created, bought, and sold).

On top of that, the ability to skip and fast-forward commercials has been the bane of television since the first VCRs were introduced. There is no doubt that brands and their media reps are getting smarter and better at capturing attention, but the format of TV advertising must adjust to this... much as it will have to adjust even more as these new trends in usage and consumption continue to evolve.

Is it a brave new world because Twitter feeds and Facebook timelines light up with mentions of TV shows? It turns out that social media doesn't really affect TV all that much.

MediaPost published another news item titled "Social Media Has Negligible Effect on TV Ratings" (October 7, 2011), which stated: "An analysis by NM Incite, a Nielsen/McKinsey Company, found a 9% overall lift in social media 'volume' a month before a TV show's start can improve numbers 1% for 18–34 viewers, who are typically the busiest on social media site[s]." It went on to cite additional data points leading to the conclusion that while social media does spread the word and helps keep the TV brands in the spotlight, it doesn't have much effect on overall ratings. In fact, this could well be the solid proof that it's challenging to make a passive media all that active and vice versa.

IS THIS MEDIA DISRUPTION? IS THIS MEDIA CONVERGENCE? IS THIS MEDIA PURGATORY?

We are mired in media purgatory since there are no clear and defined rules just yet.

New media pundits made a big mistake when betting against television (you may recall that when the Internet first became popular, lots of armchair social media quarterbacks hailed it as the death of television). Sure, the Internet has put the pain on media platforms like newspapers, magazines, and radio, but television (yes, broadcast, but specifically cable and specialty) is still going strong. Most research firms will tell you that viewership has either remained steady or risen in the past few years (and yes, I realize that younger people don't have the same affinity to the platform as the rest of the world), while advertising revenues (still a relevant metric) continue to maintain or rise (slightly).

Is this trend always going to hold up? It's hard to tell. So long as television has an audience (and fragmentation, cable, DVRs, on-demand, Hulu, Apple TV, and more have changed the game dramatically), there will always be advertisers lining up to hock their wares. Is TV advertising as relevant and powerful as it was in the day and age when it was the eight-hundred-pound gorilla, because there were no other pertinent media apes swinging along the vines? No. There aren't only three broadcasting networks that offer a very scarce commodity to a massive and captive audience anymore. And yes, the Internet is capturing a lot of the video content (and that continues to rise every day).

WHAT IS TV? WHAT IS A BOOK? WHAT IS A WEBSITE? WHAT IS AN APP?

This is going to be the real question going forward. Hugh McGuire (friend, co-host on my Media Hacks podcast, founder of PressBooks and LibriVox, and now editor of *Book: A Futurist's Manifesto*) likes to provoke us by saying that there is little difference between what an ebook is and what a website is. In a sense, he's not wrong.

The Internet was created to share documents and information. HTML, the language we use to build websites, is based on making text readable through the digital tubes. The latest evolution of this, HTML5, adds in more multimedia functionality (audio, video, etc.). If you looked at the HTML coding of the ebook for *The Catcher in the Rye* and the HTML coding for the TMZ news item "Kim Kardashian Hickey Confirmation!," along with the HTML coding for your company's website, you'll notice that they all—pretty much—look the same. What does this mean? Think about what differentiates a TV show, a movie, and a clip on YouTube. Now take out your iPad and download an episode of your favorite show on iTunes, then rent a Hollywood movie the same way, and after that watch a clip on YouTube. Notice a difference? It's all just video, isn't it? It turns out that the massive shift will be in what you do with that video.

The issue can be simplified as dogma—an established belief that we have—and it's one that few of us spend any time thinking about challenging. Businesses now have an expectation that consumers will deliberately do their social media bidding. In the same breath, they question almost anything new in terms of its validity and bottom-line impact on sales. Things change fast. In 2008, about 1 percent of trade book sales in the United States were ebooks. In 2011, that number was closer to 20 percent, and the expectation is that it will tip 50 percent in the coming year (or so). The point is that media is evolving quickly, and it's less about what you're doing with social media and more about taking a broader perspective when thinking about the media you're creating. The way to do this is to view your media as either passive or active at its core—with the knowledge that people will also do with it what they will.

Example: Aereo is being described as a service that will distribute television over the Internet (it is being backed by media maven Barry Diller—who created Fox Television and is currently the chairman and senior executive of IAC/InterActiveCorp, the company behind Vimeo, Urbanspoon, Match.com, the *Daily Beast*, and more). While the concept of Aereo is nothing new, the initial buzz around this initiative (especially if Aereo is used in combination with services like Hulu or Netflix) could indicate a changing tide in how we watch television as well.

That is, is there a difference between a TV show and a video that you watch online? We may have been looking at the new media equation backward. Instead of wondering how TV is going to adapt in the Internet age, maybe we should have been looking at how the Internet is going to adapt to TV. We all see the spikes in social media when something on TV is worth talking about (it could be ads on the Super Bowl or a celebrity unveiling a baby bump), and it's this point of media multiplatforming that exists in a world where everything hasn't melded into one channel. *Yet.*

A FUTURIST'S MEDIA MANIFESTO.

No more platforms. One platform. We're quickly moving toward a world where we simply see media as text, images, audio, and video. The truth is, the subtle differences between movies, TV shows, and video podcasts feel like they are gently going away.

It's just video—when we want it and how we want it. The subtle differences among a newspaper story, a magazine article, a book, and a blog post drift away. We're no longer putting a premium on something printed/physical against something digital/bits and bytes. It's just text (or images or audio or video)—when we want it and how we want it and then how we share it and talk it up.

Think about it this way: Once the delivery platform becomes one pipe (digital) and it's ubiquitous (you can put it on any screen you'd like), the biggest challenge for your business will be figuring out where to stick yourself into the picture in terms of marketing, communications, and advertising. Is this a trend we're going to see tomorrow? Probably not. But let's not confuse linear growth with exponential growth (a common mistake we all tend to make). We'll say things like, "Smartphones only have a 48 percent penetration rate in our country today. Based on how that has adopted over the past five years, we can expect an X percentage growth going forward." Not very likely. Don't believe me? Do some of your own tracking on the growth of iPad users from introduction to date and compare that with what the traditional analysts were predicting when it first launched in 2010 (hard to believe that it was only three years ago, isn't it?).

We have entered a world of exponential (and not linear) growth when it comes to new media. Because you can now stream all of this high-definition content with few buffering or quality issues, expect to see exponential technological improvements moving forward. What does that mean? It's going to happen a lot faster than most of us (including the experts) are prepared for. It also means that suddenly, you (and your company) are not beholden to media companies as a gateway to spread your message; suddenly you're a media publisher as well.

THE RISE OF SOCIAL TV.

We tend to forget that TV is—for most of the population—still an act of escapism (same with books, radio—which has been called "theater for the mind"—and other traditional media channels). We tend to forget this because if you're reading this book, you are active, a creator, and a doer (if you're not, you will be soon enough). This futuristic view of media as one platform is probably something you can't wait for. So as you sit at the edge of your seat and beg for your TV to become more interactive, intuitive, and available everywhere, my recommendation is that you start figuring out how to create marketing campaigns and media content that can effectively cross-channel-promote your brand, while the cable companies do everything within their power to keep their business models cash-flow-positive. Just watch and see how the traditional TV broadcasters are going to deal with companies like Apple, Google, Hulu, and Aereo as they begin creeping in to disrupt their industry (it was core to the SOPA and PIPA legislation that caused so much commotion a few years back). Much like the music industry and the book publishing industry, this is all going to get a lot messier before it gets a lot simpler.

SO, WHAT'S NEXT FOR MEDIA?

If only I had a dime for every time I've been asked, "What's next for media?"

More often than not, I do my best to deflect the question. I'm humble enough to know that my feelings of what works and where this is all going is not where we may end up. If I could see into the future, I would have created the first online auction or sold books online back in the early days; instead companies like eBay and Amazon came along first. If I knew where things were going, I would not have looked at YouTube when it first came out and said, "Who would want to watch shaky-cam videos on a two-by-two screen that has buffering issues?" (And yes, I've said stupider things—like "I don't see the point of Twitter" and "What's the big deal with Instagram" when they both first came out.)

Thankfully, I also have the humility to admit indiscretions like these, and I still spend time thinking critically about what may be coming next. In short, social media will not go away (it has become a part of the media's core fiber and how we do business), but it is time to start asking: "Now what?" Perhaps certain channels and platforms will enjoy popularity and then disappear into the ether, but Arianna Huffington (co-founder of the *Huffington Post* and current president and editor in chief of the Huffington Post Media Group) is right when she says, "Self-expression is the new entertainment."

Now that individuals are connected and can publish their own thoughts, share them, and collaborate with their friends and business peers, we are not going to return to a hierarchical broadcasting platform anytime soon. On top of that, social media is well over a decade old. Fads come and go much faster than that. Brands can now self-express as well, and that's where the magic lies.

Social media is not a market correction. This moment of purgatory is not a moment that we have seen before. Technology continually changes our landscape, and technology has dramatically changed our media. It's not like we had this technology or media before and now we are returning to it. This is new (even though it's over ten years old); the rules (if there ever will be rules) have not been firmly established or agreed upon yet. As technology continues to advance, so too will our media.

Another important note is that social media will not become all media. The next layer of social media will be the integration of the ability for all media to be social . . . but it won't necessarily act that way. Think of it this way: Just because you can make a media channel social doesn't mean that all media channels will be social. That said, if a smaller minority wants specific media to be more social, the layers and ability will be present for that to happen. And if the ability isn't there, consumers will do it on their own.

On March 30, 2012, MediaPost ran a news item titled "Facebook a Quiet Second-Screen Giant in Social TV Space?" The article went on to report that as traditional television corporations and limber TV startup disrupters attempt to create intelligent and engaging ways for people to interact with their TV through iPhones and iPads, consumers may have already decided on how they would like to socially engage with their TV viewing. Many are already doing it on Facebook, Twitter, and some other online social networking channels. What does this mean? You have to go out and "like" your consumers as much as—if not more than—you're asking them to "like" you on Facebook; in much the same way, these TV content producers must start thinking about Facebook, Twitter, and other spaces as their strategic partners in how they connect with their consumers.

THE NEXT LAYER OF MEDIA AND BRANDS.

What if television does shift to become fully interactive? What happens to all those people who just want to sit back and enjoy their favorite shows after a long day of work? Do they get left behind? What about an article in a magazine? If folks want to just read it (and not share it, highlight it, comment on it, friend it, or whatever), are they allowed to? Social media will simply be one layer added to the media mix for those who want to engage, connect, and be a part of the discourse. It will always be there as a function of the media and the desire of individuals to connect with others. It's no longer a stand-alone.

MEDIA WILL BE EITHER PASSIVE OR ACTIVE.

That's it. These are the two options:

1. Passive media.
2. Active media.

The truth is that some media will be predominantly passive (like watching a television show) with a whisper of active components (the ability to chat about it or share it with friends). Other media will be predominantly active (like Facebook); users won't get much intrinsic value unless they're active participants, but the platforms will have layers of passivity. (Think of those people who are on Twitter but aren't really tweeting or following anybody back; they're just there to passively creep on celebrities.)

This is the easiest way for you to think about your innovation in media: Can your customers be primarily passive or active with their media? What's the percentage? Can a passive media become an active media? Can an active media become a passive media? Is this what your customer wants? How will your passive and active media play together in a marketing mix? How well will your brand be able to blend the two types of media together?

WHAT IS YOUR MARKETING TRYING TO DO?

The quick answer is: *Sell more.*

We can talk about building brand affinity, loyalty programs, engaging consumers, and all of the other marketing imperatives, but if your marketing is not driving sales, it is flawed. Sorry. We can debate the merits of brand building, but without sales, there's not much of a brand.

You can sing the same song when it comes to the other critical components that make up a strong marketing mix and a hearty brand ecosystem, but it's all for nothing if it doesn't get consumers coming back for more (and telling everyone they know about it). Just ask hip brands like UNIQLO, Apple, Salesforce.com, or Trader Joe's.

MarketingCharts published a news item titled "Facebook Fan Size May Not Translate to Relationship Quality" (January 10, 2012):

> Fan volume does not appear to translate to relationship quality, though, as only 2 of the top 5 brands by fan volume, and less than half of the top 20, appear on the Fathom Research Relationship Quality Index (RQI) as of January 10, 2012. The RQI scores brands on 4 factors with equal weight: number of fans; momentum (based on speed of fan acquisition); fan engagement (based on how often they post on or interact with pages); and emotional quality (how much and how positive emotion is expressed on comments). According to Fathom Research, the top 5 Facebook brand pages, as of January 10, 2012, are YouTube, with a score of 91, followed by Coca-Cola (90), Red Bull (86), Walmart (86), and iTunes (85).

Are you shocked? This is the old "quality versus quantity" debate that keeps regurgitating itself into the marketing discourse. But it's still fascinating, as many of the more traditional marketing agencies and brands think that "winning" at Facebook is about how many people "like" a brand.

WHO VERSUS HOW MANY?

In my first book, *Six Pixels of Separation*, I engaged in the argument that it's not about how many people your brand connects to (which is the main metric that traditional advertising looks at), it's that now we can better understand who these people are and what they're really about (wants, desires, level of care).

The thinking was fairly basic: Having ten raving fans is better than blasting thousands of people who couldn't care less, and now these fans are self-identifying in places like Facebook, YouTube, Twitter . . . It seemed to make a plausible argument. My thinking has since evolved (dramatically). It's not a zero-sum game anymore. A business that is strong must have both components: a mass number of fans who are also deeply engaged. In a Facebook world of over one billion people connected and sharing, you can have both a mass number of people as well as a better understanding of who they are and what their needs are. Some fans want simple promotions, while others might want a much richer type of engagement and brand experience. The Relationship Quality Index news item above proves the point: *A lot of fans does not equal a lot of engaged fans.* And the lesson for your business is this: Know what (and whom) you are chasing.

BLASTING VERSUS TOUCHING.

Start by thinking about your business in this context:

1. **Blasting.** Shooting out messages (random or somewhat connected) with a "spray and pray" mentality is the traditional model of advertising. One big idea is advertised in multiple channels at high frequency, in the hope that the message gets recognized and acted upon after countless interruptions.
2. **Touching.** Consumers are now active with media. It's not just about seeing with their eyes, but about experiencing the brand by physically touching it with their hands. They are actively creating media about it: tweets, Facebook messages, YouTube videos, and more. The act of touching the brand usually connects them more because of the effort that takes place beyond watching a thirty-second spot.

We tend to view blasting as a bad thing and touching as the right way to market and communicate our messages. There's a commonly held belief that if you don't have engagement (and a deep one), your brand is doing something very wrong—you're simply spamming the same message into varied media channels that are all being used in the same way.

This point is true (all media channels should be treated uniquely), but it doesn't make a blasting technique (versus a touching technique) wrong. What is true is this: When a media platform is active and all your brand is doing is blasting into it a message that looks, feels, and acts like the type of message you're pushing in front of consumers while they're engaged in passive media—you're wasting your time. It's a shame because the opportunity could be that much more substantive. As excited as you should be about media being passive and active, we're going to still see many brands (and the agencies that serve them) trip up and make mistakes (another reality of media purgatory). For simplicity's sake:

- Blasting works best in passive media.
- Touching works best in active media.

BUILT TO TOUCH.

Which one is best? There is no best.

The real answer is that brands (at least, the majority of them) are not built to touch. We all marvel at how exceptions such as Zappos serve their consumers (which may not be perfect, but is very human). People care about brands and people want to be connected to brands that they care about, so if brands want nothing more than people following them so that they can blast messages at them, fine. But the truth is that there are many new and fascinating things that brands can do to capture and touch their consumers. Knowing who those customers are and getting them just a little bit more engaged seems like the ideal place to start. All of this begs the questions: What is your marketing trying to do? What is your business trying to do?

A SIMPLE WAY TO RETHINK YOUR BRAND NARRATIVE.

Many brands fail to realize that the branding game is not one of broadcasting and social media. The true marketing imperative is to tell a great brand narrative. It's a cohesive story that takes place over time and in different channels. Brands often grapple with how to integrate digital marketing and social media into their marketing mix because they're consistently working off a very traditional mass media/broadcasting mindset. Don't get me wrong, there is still plenty of time and space for traditional advertising—as we have already discussed in this chapter—to help a brand gain attention, traction, and mindshare. What we've really uncovered through digital channels, however, are more options and different ways to engage, connect, share, and grow.

Elevating your marketing to a place where you understand the balance between your passive and active media gives you the freedom to rise above the channels that are currently popular. It also forces you to focus on the business case behind doing anything. Once you've figured out your comfort levels in producing passive and active media, the challenge then becomes to figure out what you need to do next. While some brands are starting to get their wheels beneath them and better understand how to pull it all together, the truth is that all too often you have brands trying to be more social in very traditional media (think of those TV commercials that have a hue of being "social"). And more often than not, you'll find brands being very traditional (and broadcasting-like) in the more social channels (like when brands beg people to "like" them on Facebook to enter a contest).

THE SPACE BETWEEN.

If all a brand does is blast out messaging about themselves, it becomes a broadcasting model. If all a brand does is try to engage in the social media channels without ever asking for the sale or prompting their audience to better understand the business rationale behind the content they're creating, it could be fatal as well. The brand narrative (consistent and across all media) is crucial for success, and here's a simple way to start thinking about it...

Your interests:
- Why is your brand doing this?
- What are you trying to say?
- Who are you saying it to?
- What channels are being used?
- What's the point?
- How will this affect your business in a positive way?
- What is the overall economic value that these efforts will bring to the business?
- What do you need the customer to do?

Their interests:
- What do the customers want?
- What are they looking for?
- What will make them connect?
- What do they need?
- What channels are they active in?
- What do we know about them?
- What's the point for them?
- Will they really (really) care?

Your interest. Their interest...the real story lies somewhere in the middle. If it's all about us, customers don't care. If it's all about them, they may not remember us. Imagine this model as a Venn diagram, and think about that little, overlapping space in the middle. That's where your real brand story lies. That's where the great brand narratives of our time are created. That's the creative white space to focus on.

Remember: Great stories are created, nurtured, and shared over time. It's long, hard work and it only gets more complex as it starts working and getting traction.

KEY LESSONS ABOUT ACTIVE AND PASSIVE MEDIA...

Lesson #1—Define your existing media landscape.

Before creating and executing any new media campaigns and initiatives, start by taking stock of what you currently have. List everything you're doing and assign it to either an active or a passive column.

It's hard to define a go-forward strategy without taking the necessary steps to know both where you have been and how it is working for you. You may be surprised to find that while you are active on Twitter, the actual engagement is strictly passive (meaning you are simply broadcasting mass-media messages on Twitter with reciprocal engagement in terms of following people and connecting with them).

Lesson #2—Who are your consumers?

We tend to make assumptions (meaning: wrong assumptions) about our consumers and how active or inactive they may be. I've been in meetings with pharmaceutical managers who insist that the health care professionals they have surveyed are technology laggards. My marketing agency will go in and do its own research only to uncover that these professionals are at pace with most other industries, but because they are lacking both the tools and education within their profession, they're not actively using these tools and devices at work. You have to push beyond "knowing consumers" into an area of better understanding how technology affects their lives and how they use and connect with technology in everything they do.

You'll wind up uncovering some interesting universal truths. Things like: Most people try to avoid technological interconnectedness at work, but tend to embrace it in their outside, social lives. They'll spend their days chatting with their kids and checking out hotels for an upcoming trip on their smartphones. These people don't sound like laggards at all. *Asking consumers how they want to be contacted is not the same as asking consumers how they stay connected.*

Lesson #3—Getting to the active.

Using active media will look, feel, and act differently from anything else you have ever done to market your business. You're going to have to spend some serious time at understanding both how active media works and how you can contribute to it. At the same time, you're going to have to look back and figure out just how active your consumers are (and where they're active) as well.

Bottom line: You need to become more active with your media. If your business is on Facebook, Twitter, YouTube, or whatever, you have to step out of your traditional mindset of broadcasting and start to better define how you're going to transition your brand to be more active. As an example look at how businesses like Zappos, Whole Foods, and 37signals connect, communicate, and share with their customers.

Lesson #4—Active media is fast, easy, and free...

Bear in mind that it takes a lot of time to build trust and credibility. Just because you are active does not mean that your customers are ready, willing, and able to reciprocate.

If you go back and review chapter 2, "The Trust Economy," in *Six Pixels of Separation*, you'll note a section titled "In Praise of Slow." While that was written in 2008, it is just as true today when we discuss active media as it was back then. Active media is about creating real interactions between real people. It's about building real relationships that count. From that slow build (and yes, over time), comes unbridled loyalty. Yes, joining Pinterest is free, fast, and easy, but turning it into an active and valuable media channel for your business will cost you a lot of time and effort. It is not only hard and slow, but something that you (and the business) must commit to. Always keep that in mind.

Lesson #5—Appreciate the purgatory.

Purgatory is a moment of transition, but one that we can't necessarily define by time. How long will this media purgatory last? Who knows? Do we sit idly by and wait for it to pass? That would be a massive mistake. Moments of purgatory are moments of power as well. There are many businesses that are leveraging this moment—when we've been through so much and the future has yet to be established—to morph and to evolve how they connect. Appreciate it. Instead of shaking your head and wondering what happened, stop and realize that you can now have amazing direct relationships with your consumers; indeed, the opportunity is right in front of you to provide them with true tools of utility to foster long-lasting connections.

THERE'S A BETTER STORY FOR YOU TO TELL.

Let every other business worry about purgatory. Make the decision now to have a digital-first posture. Know that your consumers are way farther ahead than most of the media companies, or appreciate that if they are lagging behind, you now have a vision for how the majority of people will connect with the brands and the media that they love. We can debate the merits of which media platforms will inform consumers best, but the true value in that discourse is in deciding and acting upon the myriad of opportunities they afford you. Let others worry about the return on investment that mobile marketing will yield when compared with television advertising. You should focus on creating media that is active and passive and serving your consumers as appropriately as possible.

Now you just have to figure out who they are and what they're doing . . .

CHAPTER 4

Sex with Data

The shift from analytics, data, and consumer intimacy to brand-consumer marriage.

FROM MAD MEN TO MATH MEN.

In four words: *We are not prepared.*

Each year, we spend a chunk of our time getting organized and planning for the coming year. While some businesses are bold enough to create five- and ten-year plans, the majority of us are quite content if we get our next year's planning done (and we're even more thrilled when we actually deliver on it).

The smarter businesses are looking for specific "moments in time" to create a true impact. These are moments like product launches, a holiday season, or even a specific milestone for customers. We couple that with our brand requirements, sales goals, and beyond to build a proper business strategy that can be pushed through an effective marketing mix. Once we firm everything up, we lock in our budgets, press the button, and it's all systems go . . . or is it?

For the past few decades, businesses have been leveraging the power of data to remove more and more of the guesswork that comes with our work. Direct marketing played an integral role in helping marketers to understand the power of data, analytics, outcomes, and predictive modeling. Loyalty programs help marketers understand who their customers are (and what they are doing). Web analytics push this even farther, helping us deep-dive into the customer sales funnel and providing us with amazing insights that could be turned into "actionable outcomes" (as my friend Avinash Kaushik, the Digital Marketing Evangelist at Google and author of two bestselling business books, *Web Analytics: An Hour a Day* and *Web Analytics 2.0*, says). Now comes the magical moment when we can push beyond customer intimacy because of this data and start getting to the good stuff.

Suddenly we are able to see a lot more information (from usage to customer service issues, innovation opportunities, and advertising performance), and it's happening live and in the moment. It's now. It's not data today from usage over the past week. It's right at this very moment. In the moment.

How are you dealing with it? Probably not very well. But don't let that get you down. Even the more sophisticated businesses don't have the right tools and dashboards to do more than knowing and seeing that something is happening. There are an elite few who have pushed this information beyond the cutting edge, but they sit in the minority. The truth is that most businesses are still reviewing data and planning on a quarterly basis and—if they're really good—only looking at performance on a weekly (sometimes monthly) timeline.

It's somewhat surprising that marketing optimization is still not a massive priority for most brands, but what's even more surprising is how few of these companies have both the staff and the infrastructure in place to engage with us in real time. The raw truth is that businesses can finally react on a moment's notice to an opportunity or to something that isn't performing at the anticipated pace.

Sadly, those same businesses are too busy looking at Excel charts and reports that lie in an inbox or are stacked up on the chief marketing officer's desk. This new world, littered with amazing data, fresh information, and cool insights, has collided with a corporate world of printouts, reports, and stacks of files. They are diametrically opposed in terms of efficacy. The result is that businesses don't perform as well and wind up leaving lots of opportunities (and money) on the table for their competitors to grab.

LET'S GET IT ON.

There is a ton of confusion right now about data, what businesses are doing with it, how consumers view this as a potential breach of their privacy, and what certain companies are doing to dig a whole lot deeper into consumer behavior. We have to remember that during these moments of purgatory, everything is up for grabs. The concept of "big data" is a prime-time issue.

According to Wikipedia, "the world's technology per capita capacity to store information has roughly doubled every forty months since the 1980s (about every three years) and every day 2.5 quintillion bytes of data are created." You don't have to be Sheldon on *The Big Bang Theory* to know that this is an unwieldy amount of data, and that we simply do not have the proper tools to manage and work through all of it. While the challenge of big data is being dealt with from everyone like the usual suspects (Google, Oracle, etc.) to new and existing startups (like Kaggle), it's easy to see that as we capture, store, search, share, analyze, and visualize this treasure trove of data and usage, everything we know about business could well change. Again. And again.

So where do you start? The primary theory behind sex with data is about looking at the information that you're currently gathering (or not gathering) in a new light. Chances are that your data is coming at you in two very distinct formats:

1. **Linear data.** Most of the data that you're collecting is fairly linear. For example, you add an email address to your database, send off a promotional email, and get some kind of response. Recipients either click on something to get more information or—if you're really good—to actually buy something. For the record, if they do nothing, the act of ignoring you is also an action (albeit not the kind that you want). You then take all this information and analyze it. Think about how the entire transaction flowed. It is very linear. The same can be said for the majority of your other initiatives (be they traditional advertising ones or some of the online ones). You create and publish a message, the people who see it react (or not), and your business is delivered a data point. To date, the data that we capture and analyze has been very linear.

2. **Circular data.** Suddenly we're being inundated with tweets, friends, followers, +1s, likes, comments, questions, ratings, reviews, lions and tigers and bears, oh my! Monitoring the chatter of social media is nothing new. But this data is not linear at all. It's not based on clicking on something. It's not based on seeing and taking action on something. All this information is driven by semantics (the natural language that we all use). While there are many great paid and free tools to help you monitor and act upon the requests and moments of engagement that consumers are having with brands, it's still a much more complicated landscape to both understand and act upon. Because there are so many people making so many requests and asking so many questions through digital channels, the Internet has become one of the most powerful lead-generation tools ever created. The problem with this statement is not only

that most brands don't know what to do with the information, but even if they're acting on it, there's no simple and easy way to tie it into linear data.

GETTING DOWN TO IT!

Expect these two varied data flows to collide...and this is where the good stuff (the sex) starts to happen.

Imagine being able to not only see the linear data of how people who have opted in to your service, but also to connect it to who they are, because you have these relationships in places like Facebook and Twitter. Granted, it's not easy to make these two worlds collide, because most of the online social networks offer limited (if any) access to the true analytics. Still, having those linear and circular data points collide is the world of the future. Currently, some companies are offering rudimentary ways to gather and manipulate some of this data in fairly engaging dashboards, but the true sex with data is just around the corner.

So how do you get down to it? You not only need permission to be gathering data from your key customers, but you need to get active in the process of fostering, nurturing, and creating better dashboards and reporting for this new world of data with a plan to do something tangible with it.

Odds are that your business needs to completely reboot how you set up and measure performance based on the linear and circular data that flows. This also includes a quicker pace and desire to get things right with an iterative (or ongoing) process in lieu of post-performance analysis to get it right the next time around. At a more macro level, the only way to really improve is for you and your business to become better and closer partners with your marketing agency (or your marketing people).

A true marketing partnership over a provider or supplier mindset is what will, ultimately, really move the needle. Yes, the creatives and the strategists now need to make the data and math folks their best friends. Google holds an annual and private event for media professionals called Zeitgeist, which I am privileged to attend. At the 2011 event in Phoenix, Google chairman Dr. Eric Schmidt told the audience, "In God we trust...everyone else must bring data."

Smart. Very smart.

HOW AMAZON IS HAVING SEX WITH DATA (WHILE NO ONE IS WATCHING).

When digital mingles with our physical lives, everything changes.

The way I buy books has changed dramatically in the past few years. I used to love my book collection. I loved it so much, I would sometimes buy both the hardcover and paperback versions just to support the arts (and the authors). But after my last house move, I stopped loving my book collection. The packing, the weight, the organizing all seemed very antiquated to me.

My current book reading is done on an Amazon Kindle. When I'm in transit, I use the Kindle app on my iPhone. I hardly use my iPad anymore as I travel with the MacBook Air and I don't like reading books on that type of computer screen (just yet). I often peruse the Kindle and iBooks apps to see what's new and exciting. All of that said, I still love heading into bookstores to flip through the books and wander the aisles. When I've made my purchasing decisions, I'll crack open the Kindle and iBooks apps on my iPhone and buy my books—right then and there—in digital format. Being a retail creature of habit, I realize how bad this is for the brick-and-mortar retailer (I'm using their store as nothing more than a showroom), but the truth is that reading, buying, and storing my books in the cloud trumps all. Like other industries before it (and like the many others stuck in purgatory), retail is going to have to change. Amazon may be forcing this change faster than anyone suspected. If you don't believe me, just look at what happened to Circuit City in 2009 and then what happened to Best Buy in 2012.

It seems like the bad news that Best Buy was posting was happening at around the same time that Amazon made a lot of noise by releasing a mobile app called Price Check. If you're looking for an example of sex with data, this project is a great indicator of what will soon be possible.

The Price Check app allows consumers at the retail level to use barcode scanning, their camera, or speech-to-text search to price-check and compare with Amazon (and their merchants). Imagine the possibilities here. Once again, Amazon is changing not only online shopping but the entire retail experience. I am a huge fan of the Amazon Prime loyalty program, because it not only allows Amazon to build a very strong and targeted loyalty and analytics platform, but also turns every purchase into an impulse buy. If you can have something shipped as fast as possible to you and can still return it—no questions asked—then the retail game changes.

Price Check does this as well. It forces retailers to pay attention to their pricing. Retailers know that everyone now has a price gun on their smartphones, and that price gun is plugged into one of the largest and most aggressive retailers in the world. It also forces retailers to think differently about their in-store experiences. If a better price can be had somewhere else, there needs to be more . . . a reason to keep on coming back. We can hold up the Apple retail experience as a golden child in this instance simply because they rarely put things on sale, and their environment is not crowded with merchandise. Instead, Apple's retail experience is much more about creating a direct relationship with consumers than it is about selling them something.

The Amazon Price Check story is fascinating because it caused a public relations flurry when it was first launched. Retailers were freaking out. "How dare Amazon grab my customers away when they're finally here on my retail floor?" Amazon infuriated retailers even more by offering a 5 percent discount to those who were using their Price Check app at launch. Not only is Amazon able to beat retailers' prices because they don't have a brick-and-mortar infrastructure and because they have a different tax situation than physical stores (which are dealing with local sales taxes and the like), but now they're able to be with *all consumers in every store.*

THE GOLD IN THE DATA IS IN THE SEX WITH THE DATA.

Amazon is not hiding how they benefit from Price Check either. They are in it to capture data, and this particular kind of data set is pure gold. As millions of people use Price Check (and if you have a smartphone, why wouldn't you?), imagine Amazon's growing understanding of the market and pricing (by location right down to consumer) in terms of which stores are selling a product at a particular price. They're also better able to understand consumer buying habits and trends in real time. Who else will have this kind of data and access?

As Price Check matures and takes hold, at the macro level, Amazon will understand buyers and buying habits unlike anyone else. But it's the convergence of their linear data with the circular data where this gets very interesting. In order for consumers to use the Price Check app, they must be linked to their accounts. This means that Amazon now has all of their personal data, all of their previous buying history on Amazon, and all of their browsing as well (don't think that Amazon doesn't store what you're looking for and never bought on their site). They're also able to see if you looked at things like customer reviews (or if you have written any). They're coupling all this personal information with everything you're now doing at the physical location with Price Check.

Take a step back from this example and give yourself pause to think: What doesn't Amazon know about you at this point? They know everything . . . and you love them for it. Here's the truth: You would think that there would be some kind of privacy backlash, but people who are signed into their Amazon accounts and begin the process of shopping there tend to love all of the recommendations and social shopping functionality that the site offers. It's not uncommon to hear people lament over other e-commerce experiences by saying, "Why can't they be as good as Amazon?"

But there's a price to be paid that not all consumers understand. Keep reading.

WE HAVE TO EDUCATE CONSUMERS.

What you need to always remember about the Internet is the exact same thing that we need to educate consumers about: *The Internet is a business.*

Twitter, Facebook, Google, and the like are not social organizations created to advance the greater good. They are for-profit businesses and they are corporations. Their main focus is the same: They are here to make money. While they may have other lofty goals (connecting all human beings or helping people to share ideas), they are not charitable groups. On top of that, there is a reason why they are all free. There are no free lunches. When they give you the service for free, they need to make money some-where, and more often than not it's from capitalizing on your data (or using the consumer as a media target).

Before signing up to any service, you have to agree to their terms of service. Simply put, this is a legal document created so that the company can't be sued...for anything. It's a document to protect the company (and in doing so, it does not provide that much protection to the consumer—that's you and the brands you represent). While some of these agreements have a more fair and balanced approach (for instance, Twitter will notify you if gov-ernment or police have asked for your data), many companies are simply looking to cover their own assets. On top of that, because these channels are ever-changing and evolving, so too are the terms of service. This is a "buyer beware" scenario.

Your content is (probably) yours. While you retain the rights to the text, images, audio, and video that you post online, always consider that the content is now public and sharable forever. We've seen this evolution in platforms like Facebook. As Facebook continues to grow in popularity, they are opening up the informa-tion of their users to more and more people. Originally, only the people you were connected to (and agreed to connect to) could see everything you posted, but as Facebook attempts to gain more members (which equates to more money and advertising opportu-nities), they will continue to "open up" people's profiles. Contrast that with Twitter, where everything you tweet (from day one) is available for all to see regardless of who you are following (and who follows you).

While there are many ways that online social networks make money, there are really only two basic overall strategies:

1. **Advertising.** They sell the value of the network (the size and reach) along with the personalized data (geographic, psycho-

graphic, etc.) to advertisers, who can then send those users more targeted messages.

2. **Acquisition.** They are looking to grow the company to the point where it becomes a valuable acquisition property, and then sell the company (and all the data that comes with it) to another company (think of the $1 billion that Facebook paid for Instagram in April 2012).

In both instances, you have to be aware that your data is never in the hands of just one group, and that their intent is always to share this data to make money. It's out of your hands.

There are countless groups of people trying to fight everything I've written about above. These people feel like they have proprietary rights to their data and information and should have choices in terms of what their data is being used for. In a perfect world, I'd love to agree, but if you go back to point number one above, this is all about business.

Users and brands have to know and always remember that these services are free because they are looking to make money from the information that comes with usage. This is the social contract between the service provider and the users (take it or leave it). While complaining and petitioning might change certain aspects of a business, it will never sway companies from making money or growing their data sets.

THERE ARE NO "COPIES."

Thinking about your content (words, pictures, and videos) in terms of someone else having a "copy" is a mistake as well. This is the same mistake that many traditional organizations made when looking at WikiLeaks. There are no copies. The picture you have on your camera that you then post to Facebook is not a copy in both locations. There is a second original version that now exists in another place. The same can be said of everything digital—from your text messages and emails to your tweets. You can't have privacy online using the same definitions we used in a pre-digital world.

If you want privacy on any digital channel (and this includes your own email!), don't be a part of an online social network. It's just that simple. Even if you're comfortable with the current privacy settings in places like Twitter, Facebook, or Pinterest, be very aware that they can change at any moment. This shouldn't scare you. It simply is what it is.

In *Six Pixels of Separation*, I have a section called "Resign Your Privacy." The fact remains: There are tremendous business and professional development opportunities to chase by engaging in digital channels, but you have to be aware that they do come at a price. That price is that your information is now public, sharable, and being used by other companies to understand how you interact with the channels, who you are connecting with, and the content that you are creating and sharing, in order to better segment your data so that it can be monetized.

YOU ARE BEING FOLLOWED.

What kind of experience do you want? Marketers have abused the anonymity of IP addresses for too long, and now consumers (and journalists) are fighting back...and they're fighting mad. Everything you say and do online can and is being used against you in the online world.

Think that Gmail is free? No, it is not. And, while Google is not "reading" your email, it is scanning the content and delivering relevant advertising to you based on that. Don't like it? Go and get yourself your own email server and hosting provider and you won't miss a beat (except you're going to have to pay for it). Want more features and functionality on Facebook? What are you willing to pay? Nothing? Do you think that Facebook is a public service...or a business? In case you're not sure, take a peek at what that Facebook IPO looked like. What do you think all of these investors were buying into? (Hint: *It's your data and information*.)

As part of the TED conference in 2012, Mozilla's Atul Varma introduced a new platform called Collusion that helps individuals using the Firefox Web browser track the trackers. The initiative was created after Varma tracked who was following his young child online. After a couple of hours, it was hundreds of companies. What do all of these trackers want? Ultimately, these trackers are trying to put an advertisement in front of you that will make you take an action.

Here's a typical scenario. The other day I was looking at some different styles of shoes on Zappos but didn't buy anything. A few days later, I started noticing banner ads featuring the shoe I'd been looking at and some other styles. A couple of days later, another ad, but now with a call to action for free shipping. In its mildest form, this is what tracking looks like. The marketers call this *behavioral targeting*.

The idea is simple: If you know someone is looking at something, why not show them a relevant ad instead of a random one? It's not only a smart marketing strategy, it's a better user experience as well. People often lament advertising, but what they really don't like is untargeted messaging.

The trick is in finding the balance. How do you deliver relevant and contextual advertising (or even content), while not freaking out consumers that every click and word is being tracked and monitored, so that their web experiences can be personally optimized? Google (and other search engines) now serve up relevant search results ahead of the organic search results. In fact, many search engine optimization experts will tell you that there is no longer any true, organic natural search result: My search results are not your search results, and everyone gets their own personalized set of returns from a search query.

So in a world where all of this personalization lives and breathes, how will the two worlds of creepy tracking and ideal experience blend and come together?

IT'S ABOUT PERSONALIZATION...NOT PRIVACY.

What does purgatory look like when it comes to data, privacy, and how people feel about the online world? It's simple: Ask people if they want to be tracked and they'll instinctively tell you that you are invading their privacy.

That seems fair enough, but it isn't. If you look at any survey or study over the past decade about consumers and their relationships to advertising, you will read a very common result that transcends everything. When average consumers are asked what type of advertising they would like, the answer is always the same: *They want their advertising to be personalized, relevant, and highly targeted.* They do not want advertising to waste their time, and they do not want to be bothered by offers that are not related to them.

EXCUSE ME?

Yes, more purgatory. How are businesses supposed to deliver any level of personalization without knowing what consumers' habits are? This isn't a question of basic privacy principles. We're talking about the people who have already opted in (whether or not they have taken the time to review the terms of service agreements is a whole other ball of wax). Where does this bring us?

Consumers want personalization... but they also want to maintain their privacy.

Let's face it, we tell things to a search engine that we don't even tell our spouses or families. You're kidding yourself if you think this information (positive, negative, or neutral) is not being tracked and stored. Then again, who wants unrelated advertising flashing and bleeping across our screens? In the world of tracking, I'd much prefer that the Web is capturing everything I'm doing to deliver more relevant content to me; I just want to rest assured that this information can't be tracked back to me as an individual, right?

If a business has only my habits and trends but none of my personal information, please track away (unless this is like Amazon and I'm fine with linking that information together for a more complete experience). If the world needs a "do not track" button, we're already poised at the top of a very slippery slope.

The idea of sex with data actually makes this a magnificent time to be in business. What with Web, mobile, touch, social media, and how this all integrates into traditional marketing and communications, there could not be a more fascinating time to be in business and connect with your customers. But if we botch this, lose the trust of consumers, and do stupid things like track people down to their personal information without consent, we're not only going to screw this up, but we'll end up in a deep, dark, and evil place that we—as an industry—may not be able to get out of.

ENDLESS AISLES.

Last year, I was in New York City giving a presentation at the National Retail Federation's BIG Show event. I was part of the Shop.org First Look series and talked about the massive changes that retail will face during this purgatory.

During my time in New York City, I had the opportunity to drop into the UNIQLO store on Fifth and 53rd. It is a sight to see if you're into retail, commerce, fashion, and a unique in-store experience. I found two styles of jeans that I really liked, so I bought two pairs. The truth is that I would have bought a couple more, but they were out of my size.

What if there had been a simple touchscreen that allowed me to buy those jeans right then and there? They could be sent to my home or hotel (depending on availability); or the screen could let me know when I could come back to the store and pick them up. Seems simple enough in this day and age of e-commerce, doesn't it? Pushing that idea farther, I should be able to conduct that exact same kind of transaction from my smartphone, right?

I realize that these types of simple integrations are few and far between when it comes to retailers (and other businesses), but the expectation as a consumer is pretty straightforward—I can order online, so why can't I order online while I'm actually in the store? Attribution is a hotly debated topic when it comes to the world of retail meets digital and converged interactions (doing e-commerce from the physical store). Think about how that type of transaction may help retailers better understand both consumers and the analytics behind who in the corporate food chain gets awarded the "sale."

The sad part? In such a competitive world, they lost a sale that would have been 75 percent pricier than what I bought (had the retailer simply had the inventory). But this type of digital commerce will reshape the entire data and analytics landscape as well. Every store is limited by their footprint and historical sales to drive inventory control. No more. If you think about this integration of e-commerce at the retail level (be it on a smartphone or a touchscreen installation), retailers may discover that a store in Sioux Falls sells as much inventory on certain products (or maybe more) than a flagship store in Times Square.

Thinking that e-commerce kills the retail experience is simply bad thinking. People still like to go out, wander the malls, touch and see what's new and exciting. It's not a zero-sum game. The smarter retailers are going to wake up and realize that e-commerce will no longer be a vertical business within their retail experience... it's going to quickly become horizontal across the organization. The digitization and ability for consumers to hit the retail level, but have access to the full inventory (and maybe even more products...some of which can even be virtual goods), is going to be the true shopping experience of the soon-to-be-future for retail. It's something that would have never even become a consideration had the notion of sex with data not come to fruition. This is another example of where the linear data melded with the circular to create new levels of economic value for the company.

LESSONS FROM SEX WITH DATA...

Lesson #1—Nail down the linear.

If you don't even have the basics down on what you can (and should) be tracking, please stop everything and either get yourself more informed or bring on some help.

The traditional practice of throwing money at marketing opportunities and then trying to figure out if they have worked has come and gone. If you're not sure where to start, I highly recommend the books *Web Analytics: An Hour a Day* and *Web Analytics 2.0*. Both books are authored by Avinash Kaushik (the Digital Marketing Evangelist for Google). And his amazing blog, *Occam's Razor*, also features tons of in-depth but easy-to-read posts about everything you will need to get started, including how to figure out the economic value of a user and how to track that as a core metric. If you're not measuring and optimizing the linear data, you are already lost in the woods.

Lesson #2—Nail down the circular.

If you're not overly active in the social media sphere, make sure to (at least) secure your space by signing up for those media where your consumers are more active and start listening in on the key chattering. You will quickly be able to identify both who the key players are and what the key messages are.

There is no doubt that if you're all but ignoring these spaces, you are missing a tremendous opportunity to build your business and to become more aware of your industry.

Lesson #3—Start making out with your data.

The majority of corporate executives from small, medium, and even large businesses are struggling with data and consumer intelligence as much as the next person.

You may be surprised to hear this, but most companies would admit that they don't even know who their most loyal consumers are. It's very hard to reach those people and to build a substantial relationship if you aren't even aware of them. This makes retention a very difficult proposition.

Start small and build some dashboards. Start leveraging some social media monitoring tools and figure out how to create a unified dashboard. The idea is to tie the database that you have into the social sphere so that you can better understand your consumers and their needs.

Lesson #4—Everything is mobile.

Amazon's Price Check app turned every retail competitor's store into a showroom for Amazon. It won't just be Amazon that will be leveraging these hyperconnected consumers and their desire to connect more to brands wherever they may be.

Amazon's app enabled human beings to become data collectors for Amazon. These consumers are giving Amazon the inputs needed for success. They're collecting them and giving them over for free. Traditionally, these data points and inputs were gathered at a great cost to business. No longer. In all likelihood, Amazon is sharing this information with their partners to get better margins and grow the overall business.

Lesson #5—It's going to get strange.

While most companies can't even fathom connecting their linear and circular data, there are many new (and somewhat scary) analytical tools that will be finding their way into our lives.

It may sound like science fiction, but some of the bigger brands are currently experimenting with serious hardware to better understand what would trigger a Pavlovian response in the consumer. Yes, they're actually using advanced scientific technology to map your brain so that they can blow your mind with stuff you truly want. At the SXSW conference in 2012, Paul Saarinen (from the agency Yamamoto, based in Minneapolis) and Dr. Scott Fahrenkrug (from the University of Minnesota) presented a session titled "Influence: It's in Your Genes" that looked at DNA analysis (not joking!).

Imagine being able to market to an individual's specific DNA tastes and needs! While none of these scientific explorations is at the point where the cost is sustainable, it is becoming abundantly clear that technology, medicine, and the data that we all create on a day-to-day basis are quickly coming together to create the ultimate in personalization. As strange as this may sound to you, we need to ensure that none of this comes at the cost of consumers feeling their privacy has been violated.

Lesson #6—Technology rules.

Gartner Group reported that "by 2017, a CMO will spend more on IT than the CIO."

Let that concept marinate in your brain for a moment. This means that big data is coming to marketing, and the insights that we will soon have available to us—at the business level—will make what we're spending on computers, servers, and capital infrastructure pale in comparison.

This will finally give us true knowledge of what it takes to acquire customers and keep them. Consumers are already demonstrating their desires in this area by using their smartphones to do everything from scanning QR codes to sharing their experiences with their peers on Facebook and Twitter. When you combine their usage (the linear data) with the circular data (what they're doing in their social graph), and with all of this new big data trending information, it's easy to see how much this will affect everything we know about connecting to our consumers.

BE ACCOUNTABLE TO YOUR BRAND.

Imagine a day when you could have all of the data and analytics you have ever wanted. Imagine being able to track and analyze the journey of your consumers. Imagine being able to be a fly on the wall for all of their conversations with family and friends about what they love and hate about your brand, the competitors, and the other brands that impact their lives. Imagine being able to speak directly to them and to get their feedback. Imagine being able to test your creative output in a live environment and see which of your messages actually resonates with an audience. Imagine being able to create as many layers of engagement with those consumers as you have ever wanted.

But it's all here. No need to imagine it. You can do a lot of that right now.

Don't let the uncertainty of this purgatory hold you back. One of the main ways out of purgatory to the Promised Land will come from how you engage and connect with data in a positive, transparent, and meaningful way. Most brands will mess this up. You don't have to be one of them.

CHAPTER 5

The One-Screen World

The shift from four screens down to one.

THE ONE-SCREEN WORLD.

It was hard to tell what, exactly, you were looking at when you approached the tracks at the Seolleung underground station in Seoul, South Korea. For some, it looked like a massive billboard ad for a local supermarket, but the rows and rows of product photos actually comprised the latest Homeplus store.

This was not your standard pop-up store. It was a new, virtual supermarket. Filled with hundreds of pictures—everything from vegetables and pet food to noodles and snacks—Homeplus (the South Korean affiliate of Tesco) was giving people the same visual experience they would have if they were in one of their physical supermarkets. The big difference in these subway virtual stores was that the shopping was 100 percent mobile.

Homeplus is the number two supermarket in South Korea (after E-Mart) and was looking for a new and innovative way to become number one without increasing their number of stores. Because of the intense work ethic of Koreans, Homeplus decided to bring the store to these very busy people. Shoppers could download the Homeplus app, and by scanning the QR codes beneath each food item on these virtual walls, Koreans could turn their waiting time into productive shopping time. If orders were placed before the afternoon, Homeplus would be able to deliver the groceries on the same day.

Yes, Koreans are early technology adopters and have a culture that engenders this type of technological sampling, but it speaks volumes to our ever-changing world and adoption of mobile technology. Homeplus is no twelve-person startup either. They entered the South Korean market in a joint venture with Samsung in 1999; they now have over four hundred stores and employ more than twenty-five thousand people in South Korea. While the virtual shopping experience hasn't pushed them into the number one supermarket position (just yet), these virtual shopping experiences have boosted online sales by over 130 percent.

Ali Asaria (a former engineer at Research In Motion and the founder of Well.ca) was inspired by Homeplus, so he figured it was prime time for Canadians to have a similar experience. The Well.ca virtual shopping experience was launched at a busy Union Station in downtown Toronto. The online health and beauty store was selling everything from Pampers and Tide detergent to Crest toothpaste and Head & Shoulders shampoo in partnership with Procter & Gamble Canada. And while the store sounds fun, enticing, and very science-fictiony, let's face it: We no longer need a virtual mural to do this kind of shopping. E-commerce on mobile is a powerful reality (just ask Amazon or Fab or Kickstarter). In fact, it's safe to say that these types of virtual mobile shopping experiences don't just disrupt the retail industry—they disrupt everything.

HOW IS YOUR BUSINESS WORKING IN A THREE-... MAKE THAT FOUR-SCREEN WORLD?

I was speaking on the East Coast and a major media company's senior vice president of marketing was on a panel that preceded my keynote address. They were talking about "the four screens," and it stumped me. For years, I had heard of the term *three screens*—meaning TV, computer, and mobile—but *four screens* was a new one.

That same media company had recently announced a major acquisition and a significant portion of business regarding out-of-home advertising (also known as billboards). I've seen many of these traditional billboards updated to become digital and interactive, so that's what I was assuming this media professional meant by "four screens." It turns out that I was wrong. The fourth screen is the tablet. The prevailing wisdom is that smartphones and iPads are fundamentally different.

But are they really all that different anymore? As television takes on more interactive components and as smartphones touch and flow the same way that tablets do, aren't all these screens melding into one? We've seen smartphones take on a much bigger screen size, and we've seen Apple develop a smaller-screen iPad. Amazon's Kindle Fire, BlackBerry's PlayBook, and Google's Nexus 7 are all somewhere in between.

THERE'S SOMETHING HAPPENING HERE.

It's beginning to feel that the excitement and enthusiasm we all had for Web 2.0 and social media are suddenly (and rapidly) evolving (again). While we still engage with these services through a browser on a computer, it seems like the notion of a personal computer—as a fixed station—has all but gone. What has replaced it? Laptops, smartphones, tablets, e-readers—all of which are mobile, portable, and highly connected. Instead of the traditional Web browser as we have known it, we're engaging more with apps or message-driven mobile tools.

Don't believe me?

Five years ago, we used to look at our teenagers and roll our eyes. They would come home from high school, plunk themselves down in front of the television, grab their laptops, and then pull out their mobile phone and their iPod. They would quickly slip the earbuds on, crank up their music, and suddenly they were multiplatforming with four screens blaring at them. They actually looked like they were either trading stocks on the exchange floor or manning a military command center.

It's amazing to think how quickly that world has changed. Now it's not uncommon to see them—in that same plunked position on the couch—armed with only a smartphone or a tablet (and rarely both). We no longer live in a world of three screens (or four screens). We live in a world of one screen—whatever one screen is in front of you. That's the screen our businesses need to reboot and focus on.

IT'S ABOUT ONE SCREEN.

Stop counting screens. Remember, everything is up for a reboot and likely to change (faster than you can imagine). Screens are everywhere, and they will quickly become what we call "dumb clients": The screens themselves are largely useless; nothing happens until they're connected and networked. The content broadcasted and created on these screens will be dictated by your personal choice and your own creation. Trying to define the differences between movies, TV shows, and podcasts will be an act of futility, as we have already discussed.

Do you have an iPad or a smartphone? The more you engage with media on these devices, the more the lines between watching a movie rented from iTunes or a video from YouTube blur. It's just video. In much the same way I'll be reading an article saved via Instapaper but then transition to a book on a Kindle app or read an article online. It's just text. *The only screen that matters is the screen that is in front of me.*

HOW TO NOT BE SHORTSIGHTED IN PURGATORY.

There's a sad truth about mobile, though I don't want to hear it. Smartphones are becoming more and more popular, and the same can be said about the meteoric rise of the tablet (with the iPad as the clear leader). But even with all the impressive numbers, we're still looking at a penetration rate among the general population of anywhere between 25 and 55 percent (depending on which research group you want to believe and the country that you reside in) for smartphones and tablets.

Beyond this low penetration rate, it's also important to note that this small percentage shrinks even more when it comes to people who are paying for apps, downloading apps, and actually using apps (we've all seen the depressing stats surrounding this in innumerable different places).

Making things even more complex are the telecommunications companies, which are still charging confusing fee structures for mobile data. Text messaging is not the same as mobile Web, and different devices use different amounts of data (and we're not even talking about the complete confusion or price gouging that happens when you roam beyond your country of origin). Beyond that (as if that's not enough!), it's hard to get ubiquitous adoption of smartphones when consumers are locked into three-year contracts. Do you know what this all means? It's too small (and risky) for most businesses to jump on.

It's not only too small, but it seems like a speedier adoption may not be happening if all those spokes can't get the tire to spin any faster or smoother. It's hard to convince a brand to think about mobile when they just don't see the uptake and motion coming from the consumer.

It's an ever bigger challenge to stop brands from thinking about mobile as a strictly transactional type of advertising ("Ping consumers with an offer when they're near our stores!") and get them to see mobile as a consumer platform instead of an advertising channel (or to think about mobile from a utilitarian marketing perspective). The cost, effort, and general stress of transitioning their current digital ecosystems over to mobile also make it a daunting task. While HTML5 (the language that is used to program websites on the Internet) could well cure a lot of these woes by making programming to these many screens more responsive (not to mention offering the ability to drive more multimedia), it's still an expensive endeavor to get everything a brand is doing to be more "mobile-friendly" in this one-screen world. But what's the alternative?

DON'T LET PURGATORY GET YOU DOWN.

The skeptics see all the data above as half empty. You need to see it as half full and rising fast.

The reason why we should not listen to the woes of low smartphone adoption or the challenges of data charges and long-term phone contracts is because it's obvious—beyond the shadow of a doubt—that mobile is everything and that mobile is our future (and that future is not as far off as the researchers may lead us to believe). Fixed screens will simply be places that we toss our cloud-based content, marketing, and advertising for convenience when we're sitting on a couch. We must believe that smartphones (and devices like the iPad and others that have yet to be created) will be the source of our ever-growing connectivity, and that everything else will just be a big dumb terminal or a piece of glass that is suitable for viewing and hanging on a wall.

How long will mobile ubiquity take? Some are stuck on trying to figure out if this is "the year of mobile." Don't even think about absurdities like that. It's not relevant (and the year of mobile probably already happened). Be curious to see how mobile connectivity benchmarks and trends with the ubiquity of other utilities like electricity, phones, home heating, and beyond. Mobile ubiquity is coming fast (very fast). If you think that most brands still struggle with the Web, e-commerce, and social media, just wait. Mobile—and how it will connect us—will make everything else look like a joke . . . a mere blip in time.

This doesn't diminish or change what's happening for businesses in market now, but it is clear that the majority of media will (without question) be consumed and created on some type of mobile device. The question is this: Do you get going now, wait for it to take hold, or try to catch up after it's too late?

It's happening now. When I do presentations to audiences all over the world (and yes, these audiences run the gamut from business-to-consumer to business-to-business to even government organizations and NGOs), the prevailing wisdom of the crowds agrees that we're not talking about a very long event horizon. The general feeling from polling the audiences is that it will be two years (or less) before we're using our mobile devices for buying, ordering, and consuming media as we currently are with the tethered Internet.

Two years. Most of us are already planning for next year (or the year after), which means that the time is now.

WHAT YOU NEED TO KNOW.

The world is changing fast. By the time I write this book, it gets edited, published, sent to retail, and into your hands, the pieces of data that I am about to share will most likely be out of date.

Does that make them any less relevant? Hardly. And what this data indicates is that the one-screen world is not a possible trend but an inevitability that has already taken place, and that the growth continues at an exponential pace. When Apple CEO Tim Cook took to the stage at the Yerba Buena Center for the Arts on March 7, 2012, many people were waiting to see both how Cook would handle the first major release from Apple in a post–Steve Jobs world and what the rumored iPad would be capable of, as the iPad 2 was still selling well.

Beyond a smooth performance and a new iPad that featured Retina Display with a faster computer processor (dual-core A5X processor with quad-core graphics, thank you very much), few picked up on the staggering data point that Cook enlightened us all with. Apple sold over fifteen million iPads in the first quarter of 2012. That was more than any PC maker's total computer sales during the same quarter (including companies like HP, Lenovo, Dell, and Acer). In 2011, Apple had sold close to 175 million iPads, when all PC manufacturers combined shipped nearly 300 million PCs during that same year. The new iPad didn't disappoint either. It sold three million units in its first weekend alone. And iPad and other tablets are not the only indicator that we've moved to a one-screen world. When Cook took the stage again to announce the iPhone 5 in September 2012, the iPad numbers still stacked up (they were still outselling every PC manufacturer).

Smartphone usage is not only exploding, it's rocketing past PCs in terms of consumer adoption. Many technology analysts (including both IDC and BI Intelligence) confirm that smartphone sales are now twice PC sales. If that's not enough, Alex Cocotas of BI Intelligence predicts that smartphone sales will pass 1.5 billion units by 2016 (in 2011, there were about 350 million PCs and 1.7 billion mobile handsets sold).

Yes, computers and laptops still matter, but pick up a smartphone and then an iPad and look at your brand and your business offerings. How does the brand hold up within those experiences?

EVERYBODY IS BETTING ON MOBILE (JUST ASK GOOGLE, FACEBOOK, AND TWITTER).

We're all experts until something happens like Facebook buying Instagram for $1 billion. Facebook made it hard (very, very hard) to look past the billion dollars, but the deal was a testament to the one-screen world.

It's no secret that Facebook struggles to win on the mobile platforms. Mark Zuckerberg curated a hacker culture on a Web-based platform in building up Facebook to what it has become. On top of that, Facebook's Achilles' heel is photos. People post, share, comment, and look at photos nonstop on Facebook (admit it, just today you were probably creeping on someone from high school that you swore you would never speak to again). Photos are, without question, the biggest part of the Facebook experience, so when Instagram came along and managed to grab thirty-million-plus users on Apple's iOS platform (and then another five million in its first week on the Android platform), it became abundantly clear that what Instagram was doing *so* right was something that Facebook needed *so* desperately: the ability to take, manipulate, and share photos in a compelling way, exclusively through the mobile device.

The one-screen world is not about billion-dollar valuations or businesses speculating on potential business models. The one-screen world is an admission that everything that people are doing is now happening in the palms of their hands—whenever and wherever they are.

Some worry that this is another bubble. Simon Khalaf of Flurry shared a data point that may very well disabuse you of that notion: "In 1999, there were 38 million broadband Internet users worldwide. Today, there are 1.2 billion people getting broadband Internet access on their phones." The consumers are here and connected (we weren't quite there in 1999). To put those numbers in perspective, the iPhone 5 had two million units sold in the first twenty-four hours that it was on sale. Yes, valuations can get out of control and people who do not know what they're investing in could inflate the market, but we actually have a well-worn marketplace now with consumers who are buying. In the dot-com crash, valuations didn't make sense because there simply weren't enough connected consumers for these business valuations to be realistic. As Khalaf demonstrates, this is not the case today.

Twitter's meteoric rise and continued success have less to do with how many followers Lady Gaga has and much more to do with the fact that it was the first-ever online social network that worked better on mobile than it does on the Web. The sheer simplicity of those 140 characters of tweets makes it that much more workable and easy for consumers. Twitter's focus (from day one) was on connecting people as they were on the go. To this day, everything that Twitter does—from acquisitions to business strategy—is driven by a one-screen-world philosophy. Twitter is not the only one. While many people in the media and technology space chide Google for not having grown other business markets like their core search product, it seems obvious (at least to me) that Google's true attention is on the Android platform and how it will evolve. Your business may not be Google, Twitter, or Facebook, but it can certainly think like these giants.

Start asking very serious questions about how your business is connecting in the one-screen world.

IS THE ONE-SCREEN WORLD ALREADY A MASS MARKET?

Yes, I'm bullish on the one-screen world, but I am not blind. To date there has been a lot of research to negate both my personal enthusiasm and the data that Flurry, IDC, Apple, and others are enthusiastically bringing forward. One thing is for certain: The tide has shifted dramatically, and it won't be (too) long before the one-screen world is commonplace. There are a few key leading indicators that are pushing this forward:

- Smartphones are becoming more affordable.
- Data plans are starting to become more reasonable.
- The price of data plans is being built into the family cost structure.
- Apps are a major draw for new consumers.
- Media (music, movies, TV, books, and so on...) are also pushing this forward.
- Smartphones are a symbol of social status.
- People are comfortable watching their favorite TV shows, YouTube clips, and movies on a three-and-a-half-inch screen.
- Mobile is no longer about voice calls. It's about data.

It wasn't too long ago that mobile carriers didn't care about data. Their major concerns used to be voice usage and churn. But Cisco is now predicting that mobile data use worldwide is poised to grow to more than twenty times the current usage by 2015. It would be interesting to see what the prediction is for voice.

As we get more and more connected, not only do email, text messaging, and chat start chewing into the voice usage, but it's clear that FaceTime, Google Hangouts, mobile Skype, and other soon-to-follow products could make voice calls as relevant as sending a letter in the mail (with all due respect to the pains that the postal industry is currently facing). So where's the true pur-gatory in all of this?

- Mobile networks versus Wi-Fi versus telecommunications companies.
- Interoperable devices.
- Apple versus Android versus RIM versus Microsoft versus everyone else.
- Where do Nokia, Samsung, Sony Ericsson, and other "handset" companies fit in?
- HTML5 versus apps.
- Open versus closed.
- Not all devices are created equal.
- Software, apps, carriers, and the need to play more nicely together.

It's going to require a lot of painful business decisions before everything is much easier and the friction is removed for the consumer. While we're not quite there yet, we do see glimmers of hope and rapid change. That being said, we should all prepare ourselves for a lot more rebooting in the mobile space in the next few years and hope for some stability in the process (historically, this has been challenging). This is what makes people skittish, but you should not be. This should excite you and provide you with opportunity, all while it continues to freak out your competitors. Let them see purgatory as a negative.

A MILLION BUSINESSES IN THE PALM OF YOUR HAND.

If the Homeplus and Well.ca story didn't rattle your commonly held convictions of how business is done, everything we know about selling is about to get a whole lot more interesting in a one-screen world.

When you think about e-commerce, how does it make you feel? Do you feel that it's still a fairly nascent part of the shopping experience or do you think that it has matured to the point where it's not only a proven merchandising channel, but a critical function of how people buy? Last year, a very senior marketing professional who works at one of the world's largest corporations was recounting to me the story of how they saw a postal truck outside their corporate head offices in Silicon Valley, and every single parcel that was being off-loaded from this truck was from Amazon. He thought to himself: *This is what retail looks like in 2012.*

On March 30, 2012, MediaPost ran a news item titled "PwC: Even with Social, Stores Aren't Keeping Up," in which the company expects to see U.S. e-commerce sales hit the $279 billion mark by 2015. So we're talking real money and big money. Like anything else in business, with that steep growth and adoption come challenges, roadblocks, and adoption issues.

The biggest challenge? Figuring out how, when, and where consumers want to connect, order, and buy. Retail is, without question, morphing from a physical location (a shopping mall or a busy intersection of a popular city) to a state of digitization. What Amazon started is now being continued by new and fascinating online retailers like Fab.com.

Driven by analytics, Fab.com is a flash deal site that offers up products with a modern contemporary design flair. From posters and art to furniture and jewelry, it's about more than a great price (although sales can be up to 70 percent off retail) as Fab has managed to create its own brand, look, and feel that nurture a passionate community of customers (and fans). Other brands like One Kings Lane (which offers up home decor, gifts, kitchenware, and vintage finds) and Beyond the Rack are also doing brisk and growing business in this ever-evolving segment. These new start-ups are not only churning out millions of dollars in profit, but they're helping to redefine the world of retailing by bringing both immediacy and the ability to shop on the fly to the consumer.

These new and bold companies that are driven by a world of direct relationships, providing true utility and leveraging everything that we discussed in the last chapter on data in a one-screen world, are a testament to the challenges that traditional businesses face in the exponential growth of this one-screen world. With this new and hyperconnected customer—who is also highly untethered—we're able to get a crystal-clear view of where the struggles begin. Choose a favorite business that you frequent online. Now enter their website URL into your smartphone and tell me what you see. Is their experience adaptive? Does it work as elegantly as their website experience? More often than not, it's the exact website and nothing else—making it a nightmare on a smartphone or a tablet.

THE E-COMMERCE TIPPING POINT IS HERE AND NOW.

The data and the reality validate that most businesses are doing themselves a massive disservice by sitting on the sidelines and waiting for consumers to adopt e-commerce in a one-screen world.

The opportunity is for you to lead everyone else out of this purgatory *now*. Only you can make the choice to enable all of your platforms to accept the transactions and help your consumers navigate through the channels. The MediaPost news item mentioned earlier continues: "In fact, the PwC survey finds, people aren't waiting for stores, but inventing the multichannel experience for themselves as they go along. 'Because most retailers haven't yet created efficient multichannel models, consumers are working it out for themselves, using different channels in ways that best suit them.'" Just imagine—for a second—if the retailers took the lead, instead of waiting for consumers to adopt. The future belongs to selling everyone, anytime, everywhere.

Why is your business sitting back and waiting?

LAST QUESTION: DO YOU NEED A MOBILE VERSION OF YOUR WEBSITE?

No. You do not need a mobile version of your website.

Creating a mobile version of your website is like creating a website that is a digital version of your brochure. It's amazing to speak with business professionals and have them ask about whether or not they should have mobile versions of their websites. The reason you do not need a mobile version of your website is because mobile is *not* the same as the Web. From platform to technology to how the consumer interacts with the media, the only thing that the Web and mobile have in common is that they are both (still) new media. *Mobile is not a smaller version of a website.* You need to think of mobile with a completely different approach.

Mobile must be treated as a beast unto itself. There are varying devices in-market, from mobile browsers that lack a lot of functionality to smartphones that offer unique browser experiences (think iPhone and Android). On top of that, iPad and the new tablet revolution add a whole other layer of complexity to the equation. The way someone accesses the content is fundamentally different from a Web experience, but most important, more and more consumers are using mobile as the first gateway to find out about your brand. So as the one-screen world gains market share, we are quickly moving to a world where all of our connected (and interconnected) devices will be mobile (most of them already are). This will be the primary way we connect to information, one another, and, yes, brands as well.

LESSONS FROM THE ONE-SCREEN WORLD...

Lesson #1—It's not mobile.

Stop looking at your business as physical, Web, and mobile. It's about consumers, and the only thing that matters to consumers is the one screen that is in front of them. Too many business owners are focused on how they're going to split their marketing spend among the Web and mobile and touch, and it's much less about that and much more about what the business strategy should be dictating. Start surveying your consumers now. Today. Ask them how they connect with friends and information in the now. You won't be surprised to see how addicted they are to the devices that are always with them.

Lesson #2—Simplify through utility.

Great brands know how to create great utility by making their consumers' lives simpler.

It starts off with the basic information (how to find you and when you're open), continues to the more complex (what consumers want to buy and more), then on to the true opportunity (providing them with a utility that attaches them in a much more powerful way to your business). Simplicity and utility are not obvious and not easy to do (just ask Twitter). Look at the one screen as a blank screen: It's a fresh start to begin connecting in one of the most powerful ways that businesses have ever had.

Lesson #3—Mobile first. Web second.

Look at the past year and the true successes that we have seen in our new business world. Without hesitation, it is the businesses that approached the one-screen world head-on. Whether it's Instagram, Fab, Highlight, Path, or any other of the bright and shiny objects, you'll note that all of them slant toward the on-the-go experience and the one-screen-world consumer. It starts with where the consumer starts (a smartphone and a tablet); the fixed Web experience is either a driver back to the mobile experience or a mild version of what happens when you're touching, moving, and exploring in the one-screen environment.

Lesson #4—Social rules.

All one-screens must have social layers (or hooks) built in.

If it's a passive media experience, the tools still need to be there for people who would like to do more with the media. In this one-screen world (especially when people are on the go), the media will, fundamentally, be active. People confuse what makes something social. The commonly held misperception is that social media is all about the conversation. I do not believe that to be true. For social to be social, it has to be something that people can both easily find and share. The goal to being social is to make everything that you are doing as sharable and as findable as possible.

When you do this in a one-screen world, people find the brand, share it, and engage with it. When people engage with it, they are (hopefully) engaging with you as well. As they engage with something that resonates with them, they tend to share it throughout their social graphs. This makes it increasingly more findable for others. Yes, there are a few brands that are able to leverage this and have actual conversations with consumers, but those brands are few and far between. Plus, in a world of 140 characters, text messages, and +1s, is a conversation all that it's cracked up to be? If we can simply make consumers' lives better by providing them with what they want when they want it, is that not delivering more than the brand had initially promised?

Lesson #5—Fixed will be mobile too.

Does your refrigerator have a screen with Wi-Fi connectivity?

We used to laugh at this kind of thinking, but look around your house. It's not uncommon to see televisions, sound systems, and printers that are connected via Wi-Fi. People are now linking home services like their heating, lighting, and garage door openers to mobile apps so that they can be controlled. This idea of a fixed location—simply because the appliance doesn't move—has little to do with the mobility that is now being awarded to these devices to make them smarter. All of this is further proof that we're edging ever faster to a one-screen world. IDC is claiming that there will be over five billion connected devices by 2014. We're no longer talking about laptops, smartphones, and tablets, but anything and everything from dishwashers and cars to vending machines and beyond. These fixed machines are engaged, networked, and connected through the one-screen world...a world where everything is, in fact, mobile.

Lesson #6—Bigger than big.

With all of this data, it's still clear that we really have no true conception of just how big this one-screen world is (and how much bigger it is going to become).

Without edging too much into the future, you can begin to marvel at how powerful these devices will become as they get smarter, more intuitive, faster, and more connected. What doesn't your current mobile device know about you? It knows almost everything there is to know. From location...to usage...to who you are connected to...to what you're doing with all of your media.

The next horizon is when smartphones and tablets get smarter. "Context" will be the ability for these devices to anticipate your wants and desires and for them to be intuitively responsive to those needs. This notion of what the industry is calling "context-aware systems" will be one of the emerging trends in the next few years, according to research firm Gartner. Think about it this way: Your smartphone has all of your historical data and usage at its beck and call, so when it's noon, why shouldn't it be able to recommend a good restaurant to you based on where you are, the weather, what's happening in your agenda that day, who you are meeting, and—more important—what you're probably in the mood for? Seems simple enough, doesn't it?

IRL.

IRL stands for "In Real Life." People like to overshare online, to the point where we have some kind of familiarity with people we've never met in their protein forms. People often talk about meeting up in the real world once they've connected in places like Twitter or Facebook. Let me ask you this: When you're on Twitter or Facebook or blogging, are you not in the real world? When you're online, are you fake? Is your online avatar simply that: a representation of who you would like to be instead of who you really are?

As the great philosopher Popeye used to say: "I yam what I yam." People will look at me sideways when I say that online social networks are the real world. They don't buy it. They think that you can't create and nurture a "real" relationship online. Anything "real" has to take place in the "physical" world. I am typing this book right now, in the real world. I am using real-world emotions. I am using real words. I don't consider any of this virtual. I don't consider any of this fake or inauthentic. All of this exists in the real world. All of this exists in the one-screen world.

If we say that everything online is not "the real world," we are—to some extent—diminishing it, dismissing it, and making it seem less substantive than it is. Does a blog post hold less value to you than this book does because it's not on a page bound to other pages? Are you even reading this book as a physical object or on an e-reader? Don't get me wrong—pressing the flesh and meeting in person are critical. This is not about removing the human factor and the amazing collaboration that happens when we meet face-to-face. But when you're online, you're still in the real world. This is the real world. This is real life. This is the one-screen world.

Interlude

It's time to get personal.

In the first section of this book, "Reboot: Business," we learned that five massive movements have fundamentally changed everything that we know about business:

1. **Direct relationships.** Suddenly, not only can every business have a direct relationship with their consumers, but there is an increasing expectation from the consumers that the business will be there for them. It's less about simply responding in a timely fashion to a customer service issue and much more about how to build true and sustainable lifelong value with consumers.

2. **Consumers want utility.** They don't just want to be sold your products and wares. They want to connect with brands because these businesses are giving them a true utility that is adding value to their lives.

3. **Passive and active media.** We have moved well beyond the shiny, bright object of social media and into a world where consumers not only are publishers of their own content, but engage with media in an active way. Prior to the pervasiveness of the Internet, this was never possible, so now businesses

are struggling to figure out the balance of active media and passive media that they should be both producing and engaging in.

4. **The data is telling us much, much more.** Figuring out the balance between respecting the privacy of our customers and delivering them highly personalized and relevant marketing is no longer a future dream. It is here. People are constantly oversharing in online social networks and yet begging for more privacy. This paradox is only going to get more complex as brands have the ability to connect and share more with consumers through these direct relationships.

5. **The one-screen world.** It's not about three screens or four screens. It's not about the Web, mobile, touch, and what consumers are doing in their physical lives. It's about the reality that the only screen that matters, going forward, is the one screen in front of the consumer's face. We have a new obligation to be there when consumers expect us to be, in a way that exceeds their basic expectations. This one-screen world is going to make the Web, social media, and e-commerce (as we have seen them to date) look like a joke in terms of size, magnitude, and business opportunity. It's going to be bigger than most are assuming, and it's already happened. Businesses are gravely unprepared.

IT'S NOT A THREAT. IT'S A REALITY.

What are we going to do about these massive changes?

We must Ctrl Alt Delete. We must remove the fear, control, and uncertainty to prepare ourselves for what it means to work in this world. I have been struggling with what it means to be successful in business in the face of these new movements since

I attended the 2012 TED conference. As much as I try, I can't get the dinner conversation I had with Sherry Turkle out of my mind. Turkle is a professor at MIT and the author of the fascinating book *Alone Together: Why We Expect More from Technology and Less from Each Other*. With each passing day, as I get further and further involved in technology and digital media (especially after being neck-deep in writing this book), I flip-flop between marveling at this amazing new world and how it has changed business forever and at the same time watching so many people use technology in a way that is (without question) enslaving them. *Alone Together* is the kind of book that I caution those interested in new media to read, because it can be as depressing as it is enlightening when you begin to think deeply about our lives and our digital selves as the aforementioned five movements unfold before our eyes.

Does digital make life better? That was always my assumption. Technology is awesome, and it's hard not to be impressed with the iPhone and the incredible computational power we have in the palms of our hands (and how it connects us all). Turkle suggests another perspective: Do we really think that digital will help us lead better lives?

Shortly after attending the TED conference and discussing these topics with Turkle (which happened the night before her TED talk), I found myself at a party in Montreal for a new product launch. I got to the event a little early and instead of mingling, I retreated to a couch in the corner and the safety of my iPhone. There was nothing pressing in terms of emails or tweets for me to tend to; it was much more like a security blanket than anything else. I took warmth in my connectivity to it and how it shielded me from being social in public (something I'm admittedly not all that great at or comfortable with).

At that moment, *I realized that the iPhone was a better companion than a human being.* That sounds very tragic. That's not me or who I am, but that is how I felt.

I'm not sure I would have ever realized or acknowledged those feelings had I not met and spent time with Sherry Turkle. As much as I love technology and new media, it's important to think about the consequences as well. Since that time, when I have the urge to reach for my iPhone, I stop. I acknowledge that feeling and ask myself: *Is what's happening on the iPhone more important than what's happening in the here and now?*

The next time you're sitting on the floor and playing with the children in your family, and you get the urge to reach for your Android device, ask yourself the same question. Yes, managing technology is an important skill set to have moving forward, but it's only the tip of the digital iceberg.

FROM ME TO YOU TO US.

The next section of this book is titled "Reboot: You."

The five movements have happened, and their unfolding is beginning to take place now. To take advantage of them, you will have to change as well. This isn't about going out to buy the latest iPad or agreeing to spend more time tinkering with Facebook. This requires a whole new way of being in the work environment.

In "Reboot: You," we will uncover the seven triggers that you will need (these triggers are a culmination of attitudes, perspectives, and skill sets) to be an invaluable employee, entrepreneur, or intrapreneur. The next five years are going to bring about many new job titles and many new businesses. Your future will be solely reliant on your ability to be smart, nimble, and effective in a business world that is about to be rebooted. The good news is that there are no gold watches in your future. The good news is that you can reboot you.

ARE YOU READY?

SECTION 2

REBOOT: YOU

CHAPTER 6

Digital Erectus

The digital-first posture.

THERE WILL BE BLOOD.

The year 2010 was not great for business. The recession had taken its toll, and there was an air of uncertainty, fear, and even panic for some. It was hard to see friends get laid off from their jobs and even harder to see peers shut down their businesses. It seemed like everywhere I turned, something bad was happening in the business world. Global markets collapsed, the housing industry fell apart, our pensions shriveled up, and everything just seemed to be going sideways.

Still, people rarely feel bad for entrepreneurs when a business fails. They tend to think that the idea didn't have merit or that the market simply didn't take to it. Worse, they feel that it's what the entrepreneur deserves for not going to the office every day and taking a safe (but boring) job with stable pay (like they did). But what these naysayers always fail to recognize is that the people these entrepreneurs employ, all of their families, suppliers, and other businesses—all are supported by these entrepreneurs. We tend to forget that one downed business can affect hundreds of jobs...without even blinking. We also tend to forget that the greatest achievements in business and breakthrough innovations come from these same entrepreneurs.

I held a voluntary position for the Canadian Marketing Association during these very rough times. On my ascent to becoming the chairman of the board of directors, I was the co-chair for their national convention. This event is the largest gathering of professional marketers in Canada, and it attracts marketers from across the globe as well. It is, without question, the one annual gathering where we celebrate the year in marketing. But in 2010, there wasn't that much to celebrate.

In conjunction with the event, there is an invite-only President's Dinner that pulls together a who's who of the marketing industry. This exclusive event is your standard black-tie dinner fare; we usually have a keynote speaker—a newsworthy individual, or perhaps a politician or athlete. But because of the recession, there had been worries that the President's Dinner would be canceled. Wisely, the board of directors decided to move forward, but the decision was made to not have a keynote speaker and to save that budget for the association as it struggled to maintain membership levels and event attendance.

As co-chair of the national convention, I asked the board of directors if they would be open to having me ask one of our plenary speakers to address the audience at the President's Dinner for free. I figured that these speakers were in town for the event, and perhaps one of them would understand the value in giving a smaller presentation to such an esteemed audience. The board complied so long as the speaker would be willing to do it for the complimentary rubber chicken dinner.

The first person I thought of was Avinash Kaushik, the Digital Marketing Evangelist from Google. I was thrilled that he agreed (and if you don't know why, put this book down, head over to YouTube, do a search for him, then watch him go!). Kaushik is—without question—one of the best speakers in the world on the topic of digital marketing and how to measure success. After he wowed the audience with a very heartfelt plea to embrace the Internet for all of its powerful business glory, we moved to the question-and-answer period. From the back of the room, I saw one of the most prominent chief marketing officers from one of the world's biggest brands (name withheld to protect the guilty) raise a hand. I'll paraphrase, but the question went something like this: "Avinash, you are very passionate about the digital space, and we did try to make it work. We even hired a few recent graduates to handle a lot of the social media channels for us. They were young, engaged, and passionate, but it just didn't work out. What are we doing wrong?"

I didn't look back to see what Avinash was thinking—but I was suddenly angry. All I could think was that the Internet (and every positive thing it has brought us) has literally changed business forever. I was also upset that a senior executive at a major corporation thought that hiring a bunch of young people would handle all of this—that turning to the ones who are using digital the most was the right business strategy. I may be plugging in a lot of gadgets every day and flipping a lot of light switches, but I'm not an electrician. Right? Just because people use Facebook and Twitter doesn't mean that they have any understanding as to how they can be harnessed to become a business opportunity for a major organization. Yes, I was angry.

I HATE AVINASH KAUSHIK.

Why? I hate Kaushik because he responded in magnificent form (much better than my internal rant). This is what Kaushik said:

> The Web has been around forever and yet it is not in the blood of the executives who staff the top echelons of companies.

Make no mistake about it, they are smart, they are successful, and they want to do better, but the Web is such a paradigm shift that if it is not in your blood, it is very difficult to imagine its power and how to use it for good. How do you demand innovation, creativity, and radical rethink if you can't even imagine it?

I LOVE AVINASH KAUSHIK.

"I must admit up front that I am as hard-core as any evangelical born-again Christian in my passion when it comes to the Web," Kaushik continued. "The raw innovation and empowerment that a connected digital world has unleashed is the reason I lovingly refer to it as 'God's gift to humanity.'"

What is Kaushik really saying? While it has been over three years since he spoke, his message is still clearly new (and has still not been embraced by all of us who are stuck in this moment of purgatory): You do not have to be a digital native (someone who was born into a world where computers in the home were already prevalent) to embrace this moment of clarity. Instead, you need to assume a *digital-first posture*, because this is the posture of the consumers of today.

This isn't about hiring young talent. This isn't about outsourcing all of your new media needs. This is about shifting attitudes by embracing the very real reality of what the Internet has done to business. We also now need to be holding everybody within the organization accountable for their attitudes and behavior. While those are the words that Kaushik used to open up his speech (and words that I choose to live by as well), it is how you and every member of your team should be thinking as well. I'm talking about everybody from the most senior executives to the latest newbies, from those still stuck in the ivory tower to the people who answer the telephones, tweets, and Facebook posts. For you to be successful, you must have this digital-first posture.

THINKING WITH A DIGITAL-FIRST POSTURE.

In my first business book, *Six Pixels of Separation*, I recount the story of a friend who was looking to launch a retail endeavor. He was spending countless hours scoping out locations, speaking to interior designers, looking into leaseholds, and more. While the product line was (somewhat) unique, something was bothering me. When he met with me to discuss his website, all I could think to myself was, *Why limit yourself? Why stock a physical store on one random street in one random city, when you can really push online and define a global market?* At a bare minimum, a website, some search engine marketing, some basic social media chops, and a rudimentary email marketing strategy can take a brand very far. It's a true petri dish. From my perspective, the risks associated with a retail location—where you're beholden to issues like foot traffic and weather—seem so unpredictable when compared to the digital world.

It's a story that keeps getting told and keeps evolving. On December 19, 2011, *Forbes* published an article titled "College Football's Biggest Entrepreneur." The story is about Jared Loftus, a guy who dreamed of opening up a T-shirt shop next to Louisiana State University's Tiger Stadium in the hope of selling swag to the LSU crowd. "Today, Loftus sits at the helm of College District, an online college football merchandise company that fills 1,500–2,000 orders a week from across the nation. The former one-man operation is now up to a staff of twelve and has raked in nearly $1 million dollars this season. Loftus says that all profits are being reinvested into company growth."

Consumers are everywhere, but now they're digital-first. Loftus doesn't need to worry about LSU football being top-ranked. He doesn't have to stress over union strikes and other anomalies that can affect a retail store. Loftus can also sell anything and everything to LSU fans the world over, but the true message of the story is how Loftus is expanding. He's currently handling orders for over fifteen other school-specific websites from all over the United States. His stores remain open—twenty-four hours a day, seven days a week—and they don't close during the holidays either. Bottom line? Having a digital-first posture isn't just obvious, it's good, smart, and big business thinking.

Fact: We're almost twenty-five years into the commercialization of the Internet. Social media is almost fifteen years old. Usage and users have not declined; in fact, it's the opposite—each year more and more people are getting connected. Now, with the one-screen world coming on strong, connectivity and technology are core to our daily lives—much in the same way water, electricity, and heating have become. Some countries have literally ruled that Internet access is a basic human right (look to Finland and France as examples of this). In June 2011, the United Nations stepped up and announced that they count Internet access as a basic human right as well. If you do not start having a digital-first posture as core to your personal and business success (both today and going forward), you are simply not going to evolve through this purgatory.

In its simplest form: A digital-first posture means that the first place your consumers go when making a business decision is to their computers, smartphones, and/or tablets. This should be your default posture as well. These consumers may have received a powerful word-of-mouth referral from a lifelong friend over a coffee, but before making that final decision, walking into that office, or stepping into a store, they turn to their iPhones, iPads, or laptops and do a quick search to see what comes up. They're also no longer just searching on Google, Yahoo!, or Bing. They're pinging their social graphs. That is, they're asking their families, friends, and peers on places like Facebook, Twitter, LinkedIn, and beyond. In many instances, brands that don't have sophisticated social media monitoring tools can't even see this. Consumers are highly connected; they have access to information (positive, negative, or neutral), and they make their decisions driven by this digital-first posture. Remember that.

You do this as well. When your company is having an all-staff retreat out of town and you're notified as to which hotel you will be staying at, what's your next move? More often than not, you head over to TripAdvisor to see not only how the hotel ranks, but what others who have stayed there before you have to say about the place (and they've taken and posted pictures of their experiences as well). If you're looking for a new home, do you call a real estate agency first or look at the listings online? If you need to buy a new camera, do you go to the store and ask the sales associate what she thinks, or do you do some online research? When you have to buy a plane ticket, do you call a travel agent or book your flight online? You get the point. You know what this picture looks like, but can you honestly admit that you live and breathe this way when it comes to your work and interfacing with your team members and customers?

It's easy to see that this is primarily a first-world problem, but the fact remains that if you don't start to live and breathe with a digital-first posture, you will become obsolete. All industries and businesses are going through a dramatic digitization of services— not only in terms of how we sell, but in terms of how we operate as well. Without true dedication and a conscious choice to have a digital-first posture, you will face short-term strains and long-term pains. You may even find yourself in the middle of a severe industry rebooting when a more able-minded group comes together to create the future of the industry that you serve. Are the online channels for everybody (including the plumber at the corner of your street)? Why not? Since when was a business not about adding true value to the community that it serves? If that community is now anywhere and everywhere (including online, where consumers are looking for ratings and reviews or more in-depth information), what does it say about you if you're completely ignoring the situation (and opportunity)? Check out what people just like you are saying about your local plumber over on Angie's List.

BE FOREWARNED: THE MIRROR REFLECTS YOUR OWN CLOUT.

This ability to see, score, rate, and gauge a company's efficacy has already trickled down to you and me. There's a new measurement in town, and it's all about how relevant and influential you are—*as an individual*. In a digital-first world, you don't have to agonize over these scores and ratings, but it's important to be both aware of them and somewhat knowledgeable about how they work and their relevance.

On June 25, 2011, the *New York Times Sunday Review* ran an opinion piece called "Got Twitter? You've Been Scored," by Stephanie Rosenbloom, that looked at the emerging trend of brands using social media analytics platforms like Klout, PeerIndex, and Twitter Grader to see how "influential" individuals are. That's right: Brands are now turning the tables on consumers. This social media popularity contest has received mixed reviews (and continues to be a source of online discourse). "It seems so unfair that certain individuals are being offered free upgrades at hotels or free promotional flights just because they have a lot of Twitter followers" is a growing argument that you'll read online from those who don't have significant followings on Twitter (the ones who do don't seem to be complaining too much about the newfound attention and free goodies while they're being fawned over).

What services like Klout reinforce is the need to be aware of your online social comings and goings, because these ratings are public and available for the world to see (and this includes your boss, your employees, your customers, and your potential clients and employers). *Consumer Reports* rates and grades products and services. The Internet allowed anybody to comment on any company or service. Now the social web has brought this scoring and grading down to you and me.

Here's a personal story about influence and social grading: I spent close to fifteen years in the music industry. Along with that, I spend more time than I care to admit on airplanes. Those worlds never collided...until recently. Like most people, I buy cheap flights, and if things need to be changed, I approach the customer service staff at the gate with a smile and a prayer, and hope that I won't be charged the price of a small condo in Florida. I've had mixed results. Sometimes the staff will take pity on me, but more often than not I'm told that my flight fare doesn't offer me the luxury of changing without fees.

Recently, I was traveling with a well-known singer from a rock band (we're still friends). We got to the airport and realized that there was an earlier flight. I approached the gate and asked for a flight change; no luck. The singer approach the gate, smiled, and flipped his hair. The two attendants lit up and changed both of our flights with a smile (and upgrade). Here's a newsflash: The world is one big pecking order. It always has been. But now— because of platforms like Klout—everyone can see it, and each of our own personal scores is available with a quick online search.

My friend—the rock star—travels infrequently by plane. I'm a loyal customer of the airline. It doesn't seem fair and it doesn't make sense. *C'est la vie.* Klout and other social scoring indexes simply bring to light something we've all known for a very long time: It's always been about the numbers and whom we all—individually—influence. It's just that now we're starting to see where we all sit and how we're all connected. Pushing this farther, if everyone has their own media channel (because of our individual Twitter feeds, Facebook friends, personal blogs, Pinterest boards, LinkedIn profiles...) published for the world to see, why shouldn't they be subject to the same public rating systems and reviews that traditional media channels have to endure?

A DIGITAL-FIRST POSTURE IS A HUMBLING POSTURE.

The marketing industry trade magazine/bible, *Advertising Age*, has a digital platform called Power 150, which ranks all of the marketing and communications blogs in the world. On any given day, my blog will rank somewhere between twenty and thirty. Is it perfectly accurate? Who knows?

While it's humbling to know that I rank so highly, it's even more humbling to know how far I must go to crack that elusive top ten. I can think that my blog is as good as any others for marketers, but the public nature of my ranking is a slap in the face as well as a pat on the back, depending on my level of humility and how I'm feeling on any given day. And yes, the same can be said for your Twitter account, your Facebook profile, and how many people (or which people) like what you're all about—especially when it's linked to your business and how you think about your industry.

Whether we like these new tools of measuring influence or even if we grapple with the definition of *influencer*, this is becoming an increasingly powerful way for brands and individuals to better understand who they're connected to and what those groups of people do. While Klout seems to be the most pervasive of these social scoring platforms, you can rest assured that as the technology becomes more mature, it will attract competitors and the indexing system and algorithms will get better and more accurate. We're still primarily dealing with what we have previously defined as linear data when it comes to these services, but as semantic analysis tools come online, and the worlds of linear and circular data combine, scoring systems could become very accurate and very humbling.

In addition, this also shifts some of the power back to brands. As individuals kvetch and moan about how they're being mistreated and how loyal they have been to a brand, companies now have the power to see how influential these individuals truly are—and with a few simple searches, they can see who they are, what they do, and who they are connected to. Individuals threatening to call a brand out online can now be referenced to see just how much their message may (or may not) amplify and spread. Mark W. Schaefer (the executive director of Schaefer Marketing Solutions and a professor at Rutgers University) published an excellent book on this topic titled *Return on Influence: The Revolutionary Power of Klout, Social Scoring, and Influence Marketing*, which dives into this topic with much more depth and analysis. If you're trying to understand how to harness the power of your own individual clout (or Klout), I highly recommend his book. If you're still unsure as to how relevant this all is (and will be), Schaefer is quick to remind me that it's not uncommon for applicants to include their Klout score on their résumés. Deal with that.

A GOOD DIGITAL POSTURE IS A SIMPLE DIGITAL POSTURE.

It's not easier than it looks. Sorry. Not only is shifting toward a digital posture complex and challenging, the truth is that if you have been in business for some time, your ability to untangle your current business DNA, attitude, and philosophy will not be easy. You may find yourself having to reboot everything that you have come to believe as a truth. Yes, this will be infinitely easier for those who are just starting out, because there is no baggage, history, or stories about the "good old days" to overcome. In essence, what you're looking to do is to not only simplify everything, but also use the new tools that are available to you to nurture your own success. There is irony in this new posture: Getting to simplicity is not easy. It can be painful and complex. But in the end, driving toward simplicity is everything.

PENNEY FOR YOUR THOUGHTS.

No one knows the value of simplicity and the power that it brings better than Ron Johnson. Prior to becoming the CEO of JCPenney, Johnson was the senior vice president of retail operations at Apple. In short, he led the concept of both the Apple retail stores and the Genius Bar. His record at Apple is pristine. Within two years of the first store opening, the retail operation of Apple surpassed a billion dollars in annual sales (beating the record held by The Gap). Globally, Apple now has over three hundred stores, and their expansion plans continue to be as aggressive as their product launches.

In November 2011, Johnson left Apple to lead JCPenney through this time of purgatory and reboot. His first big and bold moves made news as the 110-year-old company not only struggles to remain relevant but fights within the constraints of the traditional retail world—a place where being an anchor store at a highly coveted shopping mall was the difference between success and failure. You'll note that Apple doesn't look at retail in this fashion, and neither does Amazon (which has hinted that they may enter the bricks-and-mortar fray, but as of this writing they still remain a digital pure-play). Johnson's approach to the new

JCPenney is founded on creating a much simpler experience that fosters the digital-first world where consumers are checking and double-checking products, reviews, and prices.

"Steve [Jobs] would have thought that was insanity," Johnson said when he was discussing the company's advertising history at the launch of the new, simpler JCPenney at Pier 57 in New York City in late January 2012. Johnson was referring to their promotional campaigns. To put some context around how complex things had become at JCPenney, the mass retailer ran close to six hundred promotions in 2011 (with an estimated cost of $2 million per promotion). According to Johnson, 99 percent of the JCPenney potential client base was ignoring those promotions. Johnson pared the 590 promotions down to just 12. "They're called months," Johnson joked with the media. This plan would also shift the promotions from seasonal to monthly.

The success of this strategy is playing itself out right now—before our very eyes (as of December 2012, it became apparent that this campaign wasn't clicking with consumers, and so it was being iterated and tweaked). Whether or not it is perceived as successful by both Wall Street and consumers is less important than the philosophy that Johnson—an individual who helped build the Apple retail experience—is bestowing on us mere mortals. What we're learning from Johnson and the JCPenney experience is that simple is not obvious. It takes work, and it's not always going to work on the first try. To date, JCPenney continues to struggle as it unravels the layers of complexity to define a simpler approach to business and their consumers. Instead of shrugging and concluding that JCPenney has failed, we could also take this lesson and apply it to our lives: Simple is not easy, and it will take some time and effort to strip away the decades of complexity that the majority of us have created for our businesses and how we approach them.

SIMPLIFY OR DIE.

Steve Jobs often lamented that Apple "thinks a lot about how products should be made to look pure and seamless." As great as he was, he was not the only one who knows this. Put the book down and look at the home screen of Google, Twitter, Instagram, Facebook, Wikipedia. What do you see? Not much. Why? What makes Google, Twitter, Facebook, and others work (and be successful) when compared with their competitors—or those who tried something similar (and failed miserably)—comes from a core philosophy of real simplicity. When someone asks you what makes Facebook (or whomever) so successful, simply smile and say, "The answer is simple: It's simple." They keep it clean and pristine with a laser focus.

SIMPLE + KINDNESS = WINNING DIGITAL-FIRST POSTURE.

Is it that hard to be kind to one another? It's an important question to ask. Not just in life, but in business as well. Is the simple act of having a culture of kindness going to affect the bottom line in a negative way? Meaning, can a business be both kind and profitable? We have seen instances when two seemingly diametrically opposed concepts like this have worked together in harmony (look no further than companies that are both environmentally perfect and also highly profitable). Why isn't kindness the primary directive for more (or any) companies? Why is there a business culture and belief system that those who are kind usually come in last (especially when looking at the almighty dollar)?

Here's where you (and your newly minted digital-first posture) come into play: *Companies are becoming more and more transparent.* Not because they want to be, but because they have no choice. Blogs, Twitter, Facebook, and more are pushing (and publishing) the truth about companies—and how they're treating their consumers—out into the public's zeitgeist. Not because companies want these stories published, but because consumers now have a platform, voice, publishing environment, and audience to do so (plus, it's free, fast, and easy). The conversations that were traditionally held over dinner, at the watercooler, and at the gym are now indexable, findable, retweeted, and permanently present; they can be seen by doing some simple searches or by hanging out in an online social network.

On top of that, everybody feels like they've been taken advantage of by some form of business—at some point in their lives—so these companies and brands are being called out and they're reacting. Some are more proactive than others, but make no mistake about it, this is a reactive action by companies. In a perfect world, they would prefer if customers would take their complaint and shove it (but at the same time, please keep on buying our products and services).

In June 2010, *Delivering Happiness* was published and became an instant bestseller. The book is written by Tony Hsieh—the CEO of Zappos. Most people know Zappos as the hot footwear/clothing retailer that has taken the e-commerce world by storm, or for the acquisition of Zappos by Amazon (which paid close to $1 billion for the business). Scratching a little deeper beneath the surface, you'll uncover that what really drives this profitable, likable, and media-friendly company is amazing customer service. Buying shoes seems like one of the more difficult things to do online, but Zappos has overcome this hurdle by initiating a radical (and much-lauded) customer service protocol. Sure, anything you buy is easy, simple, and carefree to return, but it's the Zappos customer service people and how they interact with their consumers (mail, phone, and online) that has really changed the game. Hsieh himself is easily accessible in places like Twitter and Facebook, but that's not the main reason for Zappos's growth. Simply put: Zappos is not just about customer service...they are a *kind* company when it comes to customer service.

In what has become the stuff of urban legend, there is a story of an individual who had a death in the family. Upon cleaning out their loved one's home they discovered many unopened boxes of Zappos shoes. Not knowing what to do, the person called Zappos. Without a receipt or knowing how long the shoes had been sitting in the closet, the customer service rep arranged to have the shoes picked up (at no charge), and a refund was made. Seems kind enough, but the individual who was dealing with a death in the family also received flowers and a note of condolence from Zappos the following day.

Now, where do you think that person religiously buys all of their shoes? How often do you think that story gets told to family and friends? How many times has that story now transcended this person's social graph to mass media outlets or to the online world or now in this book? For all we know, this is the stuff of fables and lore...but it stands tall as a lighthouse, and as an image of kindness that is core to what the business is all about.

Does Zappos get it right 100 percent of the time? Doubtful. Do consumers always feel like every brand interaction they have with the company is one of pure kindness? Probably not. Does being kind get people talking about, buying from, and loving a company like Zappos? Absolutely. What about getting people loyal to the brand beyond logic and reason? Sure thing. Zappos is the digital-first posture incarnate. It doesn't take much to win by offering simple solutions in a kind way. Did it really take this moment of purgatory for all of us to remember the value systems that our parents and grandparents tried to instill in us as small children?

Transparency, openness, and a company's ability to communicate in a real human way with consumers are quickly becoming business table stakes. If you're not listening, monitoring, and responding to people and their concerns (or accolades), your competitors will. Currently, the act of being kind to consumers is being forced on companies, and we should all look to change—not because our consumers are demanding it, but *because it's the right thing to do. Because it's who we really are.*

What would your business look like if you made kindness the main thing that you do? Imagine an airline where ticket changes, seat assignments, and checking baggage were the basic kind acts they offered their customers. Imagine if everyone, from the customer service reps to flight attendants and pilots, all treated their customers and one another the same way they treat close family members. How much more would you pay for an airline ticket like that? How loyal would you be to them?

Kindness is the main trait we look for in new acquaintances. It's what we expect of our most personal relationships. We should demand it in business. Ask yourself this: Which companies do you know that are genuinely kind—across the board—to their employees, customers, and the community they serve? I asked this question to my online social network on Twitter, Facebook, and LinkedIn. I am sad to report that there was no mention of any company that populates the *Fortune* 1000 or is listed in the annual report of the top brands in the world. The overwhelming majority were digital-first companies, staffed by people with a digital-first posture.

LESSONS FROM A DIGITAL-FIRST POSTURE...

Lesson #1—Humanity first.

When people think of a digital-first posture, they immediately think that they can hide behind a keyboard and a username. Some do, but that's not the opportunity. The people who really connect, make a difference, and grow their business unlike anything we have seen before are the ones who use technology to make them more human to others. This is important. While everyone else is still looking for a way to separate their personal friends from their work colleagues on Facebook, your strategy should be to find a way to make who you are come to life. This doesn't mean you need to start a personal blog today, but it does mean that you can make better decisions about how you connect, communicate, and share by treating your digital connections in a much more humane and sincere way.

Lesson #2—Become a digital native.

Don't shake your head in bewilderment with each release of a new iPhone. Just go to the Apple store, arrange for a meeting with the geeks at the Genius Bar, and have them give you a tour of everything new and interesting. Spend some time on YouTube looking at video tutorials of everything from new gadgets to how to use Facebook better as a business. Whenever you feel the urge to blurt out something like "I would never join Facebook" or "Pinterest seems so silly," bite your tongue. Act like a digital native (even if you're a digital immigrant). Try it, tinker with it, pretend that it's the greatest thing since sliced bread. Think back to when you were a teenager and how anything new seemed like the most exciting and important thing to you in the world. Just a little bit of that kind of approach will straighten your digital posture right up.

Lesson #3—They're ranking you.

Whether we like it or not, services like Klout are here and they are becoming increasingly powerful and relevant. Social scoring is something we all have to deal with. We need to look at it in terms of ourselves and the team members we surround ourselves with, and we need to use these tools to better understand our consumers (both the good ones and the ones that are not as kind) and how we—as individuals—are now being reflected in new media.

Lesson #4—A lesson in humility.

If you put something out there and it doesn't connect, those digital tumbleweeds and virtual crickets are telling you to have the humility to realign whatever it is you're creating. Many online channels, including Facebook, give you instant feedback in real time, in a world where everyone is striving and starving for attention. Have some humility. And remember, it's hard to hide online.

Lesson #5—Simple is as simple does.

Are you making every connection with you as simple as possible? Look at everything from the copy on your website to what the experience is like when someone tries to find you on their smartphone. Sometimes, the most obvious answer to a problem is staring at you right in the face.

Salman Khan used to tutor his cousin, Nadia, via long distance by posting videos on YouTube. This very simplistic way of working has turned into an educational movement that is shaking the very foundation of our educational system. The Khan Academy has become a lighthouse for new and different ways to think about education and how kids can learn. iTunes U allows universities to post their lectures online for anyone to download and sample.

In short, the technology is becoming simpler, but the solutions to our standard business problems have also become easier because of our connectivity (it's up to you to piece them together). You don't need a five-year technology road map to get things done anymore. You don't need a multimillion-dollar data warehouse either. You need to think about using simple tools to create more simplicity in your business. Keep peeling away at the layers of the onion. The simple solutions are here, there, and everywhere.

LEANING INTO IT.

Kindness doesn't mean that you're going to be taken advantage of—it simply means that you're going to align yourself with the right co-workers and the right customers. Embrace kindness as a core value system for your newly christened digital-first posture. Now the whole world begins to change for the better as your digital-first posture comes to resemble the great person whose friends tell others about.

CHAPTER 7

The Long and Squiggly Road

Your career needs to get a whole lot more squiggly in this time of purgatory.

HOW DID YOU GET HERE?

To be an effective business leader (and this is, without question, the goal for those of us who want to still be employable moving forward) requires you to not only personally embrace a digital-first posture but to also look microscopically at your career to date and where it is headed.

I'm fascinated by successful people and their career paths. Do you know what I never hear when I listen to a successful businessperson speak or when I read a biography of someone I respect? I never hear a story that goes like this: "I always knew that I wanted to be in marketing. There was never any doubt in my mind. All through elementary school, all I could do was daydream about marketing campaigns and working on a company's overall strategic vision. While other kids were outside playing, I was busy drawing up logos for imaginary companies. In high school, I started the marketing club and could not wait until our economics teacher touched—ever so slightly—on the topic of marketing. Right after high school graduation, I interned at an advertising agency and could not wait to pursue my MBA with a focus on marketing."

My point? Very few people set out in life to be the people that they have become. Even fewer know that they're going to be in one specific industry from a very young age. The most successful and interesting entrepreneurs and businesspeople don't have a very linear career path. In fact, it's actually very squiggly. Always bear that in mind. Embrace the squiggle.

THE REALITY OF CAREER CHOICES IN A CTRL ALT DELETE WORLD.

You can contrast the fictional story above with the tale of a friend of mine. This individual was never really sure what she wanted to do. There was no clear desire or talent in a single area of interest. In her final years of high school, a guidance counselor recommended engineering or the sciences because she had above-average math grades. So my friend studied engineering through university and squeaked by.

Never passionate about it, she got her diploma and entered the workforce. I had lunch with her a while back and she confessed that she was miserable because of her work but could not figure out why. She had followed all the rules; she did okay in school, she advanced in a field that typically enables you to be both employable and well paid. Being an engineer was supposed to be a good life. We talked for a bit, and then I half jokingly said, "It's crazy that your current life is based on a few random decisions you made when you were sixteen. Can you imagine that? What did we really know at sixteen?" Her face became flushed. She sat before me— jaw dropped—and said, "That's it! Why am I leading this life based on the decision I made as a sixteen-year-old?"

But the truth is, many of us are doing exactly that.

EMBRACE YOUR SQUIGGLE.

Here's my personal journey: From a very young age, I had a passion for two things: music and technology. My two older (and one younger) brothers were active participants in this indoctrination. From a young age, if I didn't rock along with my brothers to the music of KISS, Queen, the Clash, or the Police, they would choke me until I would comply. I guess I didn't have a choice but to love music. I came from a middle-class family; my parents were both hard workers. My father owned a pharmacy and my mother was a bookkeeper. So, while we did better than most, we certainly were not among the most affluent in our community (not even close). As a way to make her own life easier (and not break the family budget), my mother would usually buy one nicer gift for the four brothers to share instead of four small ones during the holidays. Once in-home technology became readily available, we were the family with the first version of Pong, then Atari, Intellivision, Betamax, and the earlier home computers (Atari 800). As personal computing continued, our house was (without question) a model for early adoption. I was always curious. Not curious in an *I wonder why?* way, but curious in an *I can do that!* way. I just figured if someone else could do something with a computer, I could probably do it as well.

I would spend hours upon hours reading music magazines. Unlike most teenagers who dreamed of being rock stars, I would look at articles, dissect them, and then wonder to myself, *Who is this person who gets to sit down with Gene Simmons from KISS and spend an hour speaking to him?* It sounded like an interesting line of work. I would often spend my days hanging out at record stores (remember those?), chatting and connecting to both the people who worked there and those who were scouring the same bins I was.

Somehow along the way, I met someone who was writing for a teen magazine, and he offered me an opportunity to help out (I would basically transcribe his interviews and type up handwritten articles). There was no pay, but the free CDs, cassette tapes, and occasional tickets to a rock show were worth more than any salary (besides, any salary that I made would have probably been spent on those exact things). In 1989, this individual invited me to take a road trip to Toronto because he had some interviews to conduct and a couple of shows to catch. While we were driving to Toronto from my home in Montreal (about a six-hour drive), we got a call that Tommy Lee (the infamous drummer from Mötley Crüe) was going to be in town promoting the release of *Dr. Feelgood* and was available for an interview. This was my big chance. I got to conduct that interview and write the feature. I was in heaven.

From that moment on, I was a contributor to a national teen magazine. I was nineteen years old, and for me, there could not have been a cooler job on the planet. Shortly after that, the publisher of the magazine fell ill to the point of needing surgery. After he recovered, he decided to change career paths, sell off the magazine, and walk away. But I didn't want my party to end. I realized that if I wanted to be successful, I would have to take control of my own fate.

So in a very naive move, in order to fill the void left by the now-defunct teen magazine, I started hatching a plan to publish my own music magazines. Within a few years, a business partner and I had two such magazines and supported a friend in launching a third. Around this time, the Internet was just coming online. I had already been active with bulletin board services and modem connectivity, but when I saw my first Web browser (Marc Andreessen's Mosaic) my whole world changed. I realized that the days of me walking over to the corner newsstand and hoping the new issue of *Circus* magazine was on sale were over.

Suddenly this thing called "the Internet" could send me information—almost instantly. I immediately started publishing our magazines online. At the time, this was nothing more than the text from the articles and a little logo in the top left corner of the screen. Back then, websites didn't even have hyperlinks. I don't think anybody ever saw those online articles, mostly because I don't think there were that many people online at the time.

After a few years of publishing magazines and running all over the world chasing rock stars like the kid in the movie *Almost Famous* (sadly, there was no Kate Hudson in my story), I decided it was enough. I came back home, did my best to undo the built-up anxiety of publishing magazines in the music industry, dropped some serious weight, and started thinking about my next opportunity. I wound up becoming the editor of a local magazine that featured up-and-coming young people in my local community. From there, I continued to do some freelance music writing and continued to stay engaged with technology (a theme that continues to this day).

While I was interviewing a group of entrepreneurs at a local startup, they offered me a job helping them sell online advertising. It was for one of the first meta-search engines on the Internet (long before Google even existed). To this day, I could not tell you why I accepted this job; it just felt like an interesting challenge and opportunity. We wound up growing the business significantly and went through all of the excitement and disappointment of the dot-com boom, bust, and blowout. I stayed with this company until a bit after the dot-com bubble burst and then became the marketing director for a company that specialized in creating content for mobile devices (this is back in 2001—long before anybody knew or cared about content on a mobile device).

That job lasted for about a year. I then became an account director at a public relations firm that specialized in technology and quickly realized that this was not what I was meant to be doing either. From there, I decided to go back into the music industry and started a record label with someone I had met through some old music industry connections. At about the same time, I met up with my current business partners at Twist Image and realized that digital marketing was of more interest to me than the record label, so I sold my shares over to my label partner and took on Twist Image as my full-time gig.

YES... IT'S VERY CONFUSING... AND THERE IS A LOT OF SQUIGGLE.

It's easy to look back on this journey and say that I was unfocused, unsure, and randomly jumping on opportunities; I didn't spend a lot of time in any one particular company (until I found my permanent home at Twist Image). You could also say that I was learning, growing, figuring out what was working for me (and what wasn't), and following areas of interest and intrigue. It took me meeting my current business partners at Twist Image and creating the vision for our marketing agency together for me to realize that my career trajectory was (and continues to be) a very squiggly path. The path was squiggly because during those two decades, business also became very squiggly. More than that, however, I was always thinking about people who made some decisions in high school and suddenly found themselves years later gainfully employed but miserable and unfulfilled.

Perhaps it was my rock 'n' roll upbringing that did it. Regardless, the realization is this: Some people perceive changing jobs and switching industries as reckless. Take a cold, hard look at these people in this day and age and ask yourself: *How secure are their jobs?* We live in a time where a company like Kodak can collapse while at the same time a simple photo-sharing app called

Instagram gets bought for a billion dollars by Facebook. Which company do you think feels more secure?

The answer is simple: neither. Welcome to purgatory (again), and welcome to a career that will have to embrace the squiggle.

ACCEPT IT: THERE IS NO GOLD WATCH IN YOUR FUTURE.

Here's the thing: People want guarantees. If I go to school and get a degree, I get a well-paying job, right? If I work hard my whole life, I'll have a pension, right? If I do everything my boss tells me to do, I'll get that promotion, right? I've been fortunate enough to have met some of the most fascinating musicians, artists, thinkers, authors, business leaders, and politicians around. I don't take that gift for granted. If there's one thing that has become abundantly clear to me, it's that the most successful people I know have very squiggly careers. No linear paths and no constant and consistent ascents. It's been bumpy, weird, strange, funky, and all-around fascinating.

ISN'T THAT COOL?

What I see as cool, most people read as terrifying. I can't explain why I think like this (and I recognize that these are first-world thinking philosophies), but I have never been motivated by things like promotions, salaries, or titles. Instead I'm motivated by curiosity, personal development, and a feeling of fulfillment. I was working as an editor for a community magazine when I suddenly agreed to become a sales representative for an online search engine startup. Why did I make that decision? It made no sense (it still makes no sense). I never even really liked the ad sales part of the publishing business. Yes, I was both intrigued and fascinated with the Internet, but it was risky, unproven, and I didn't have the skill set required. Regardless, it felt right. In hindsight, it was one of the best career choices I have ever made. Interesting how those squiggly lines work out. What some might call jumping around, I might call following my own professional muse (perhaps my own destiny).

WHAT ABOUT YOU?

Do you find yourself stuck in thinking that it's time to "adapt or die"? There are days when it is the soundtrack of my life—and then there are days when I shake my head at the connotations. You see, it's easy to be an armchair quarterback and say that the newspaper industry, the music industry, the book publishing industry, the retail industry, a traditional advertising agency . . . and almost every other industry should adapt or die. We live in interesting times (to steal a turn of phrase from the ancient Chinese curse), but it's not so easy to "adapt or die"—especially when it comes to our own careers. Are we supposed to go back to university or trade school?

Odeo was a startup that was attempting to become the Google for audio and video. Creating the ability to search and find audio and video is a difficult proposition, but the company was doing everything from helping consumers record podcasts to being able to share and find them. The founders, Noah Glass and Evan Williams, were moving forward with the business, but they quickly began to realize that the adoption of their offering was not moving at the pace that they had hoped. After some brainstorming sessions with the board of directors, Jack Dorsey introduced a new concept: He was thinking about how to use SMS text messaging to communicate within a smaller group of people and not just one person to another. That was the original concept for Twitter, and to this day this story acts as a bellwether example of a company that figured out how to adapt without having anyone die. Yes—from figuring out a way for people to find podcasts to creating Twitter in one reboot. Now, think about your career. What can you do today that will not only keep you employable moving forward but keep you motivated to grow, learn, and continue to serve your industry?

What this means: In a world where we need to reboot business, we must also get very comfortable that our careers will no longer track in a linear fashion. This is why the future of your life in business is about your ability to embrace the idea that it will be squiggly. It will not look the way careers looked in the past; it will twist and it will turn. Shifts and variances will often be lateral and circular. Get used to the squiggle of your career.

Do you find it easy to embrace the squiggle? It's not. Here's why: For the majority of businesses, "adapt or die" is not about learning a new skill set or taking on more services.

For example, when we say to a newspaper, "adapt or die," we are really saying . . .

- Your business model is no longer viable.
- Your current business model is becoming obsolete.
- All of your investments (printing press, skilled labor, transportation . . .) are now a liability.
- Your staff is no longer in touch with the newer business models.
- There are fewer and fewer consumers interested in what you are selling.
- Your way of doing things converted to the digital frontier does not equate to the same revenue.
- Your channels of innovation aren't nimble enough to beat a fresh startup.
- Your technology is already considered a legacy system.

- Your employees (who may even be unionized) don't make it easy to change.
- Your shareholders will not stand for a revolution. They want continued and stable growth. Not risk.

What would you do?

It's easy to say, "Go digital. It's all about the Web or mobile or social," but these are companies that have both a legacy and a functioning business model. While the newspaper business may be tarnished in this day and age, it is still profitable and keeps many people employed. Must that all be destroyed in order to thrive in our ever-changing economy? Again, put yourself in their shoes . . . would you be able to pull the trigger? To break the lease, to fire everyone (or almost everyone), to completely disrupt the business model for a new one, to begin the long and arduous process of (basically) starting over, to recruit, hire, and train a new team for this new work, to educate both yourself and those who may be able to make the transition effectively . . . and on and on?

Is there an example of a firm that didn't completely implode everything and start over yet didn't just sit back and let the evolution of business send them toward extinction? The answer is, of course, yes. Instagram started out as a very derivative copy of foursquare before switching its focus to mobile photos with a social edge. Google continues to fascinate as the search engine expands into areas like online video (YouTube), mobile (Android and the Nexus line of devices), email services (Gmail), Web browsers (Google Chrome), online social networking (Google+), and beyond (self-driving cars and Google Glasses). Amazon continues to squiggle by pushing beyond selling books online into e-readers (Kindle), selling shoes (Zappos), offering cloud computing technology (Amazon Web Services), and beyond. When you actually start digging down deep into how these companies have evolved and stayed relevant, you won't see business models that look like anything from the playbooks of Kodak or RIM. These organizations are in a constant state of rebooting with teams of people who are actively guiding their own careers as they squiggle. Even MySpace is making another run at it by being squiggly.

The challenge for you and your career is to not remain stuck in the past and to not get too comfortable with how things are today. Is it time to take chances? Absolutely. Is it time to blow everything up and start over? Maybe for some, but not for many. Is it time to kill even the profitable business units because you know there's no future there? That's a very tough call. Regardless of what we—as business owners and employees—are capable of, there are bigger forces at play: technology, connectivity, mobility, analytics, data, creativity, commerce, publishing, and more that will continue to reshape and change how we do business. So, where does this leave you and your career? Do you adapt or die? Maybe it's more like tweak, iterate, and get comfortable with the squiggle as this purgatory unfolds.

LOST IN ADAPTATION.

You will have to adapt to a world where your career can (and should) get squiggly. You wind up seeing, reading, and listening to a lot of content (both online and in traditional publications) that speaks to the coming years and what businesses should expect in terms of disruptions, predictions, new channels, and shinier and brighter objects. It's almost easier to say that everything we have known about business continues to change and that the only constant in our lives will be change. Fine. Dandy. Now what? The true adaptation for you (and your business) will not be about how smart you are with your marketing or whether or not you're doing clever things in spaces like Twitter or Facebook. True adaptation will come from how well you can get over what I call "the lazy" and move to a place where squiggly becomes your friend.

GETTING OVER THE LAZY.

Here's an example from my industry to help you create the right frame of mind when you approach whatever work you do: Marketers on the brand side either manage (and involve) themselves in an agency relationship, or they manage and involve themselves with an internal marketing team. Most see digital marketing and social media as a new channel to integrate versus a new layer that lies at the foundation of all marketing initiatives. While there are some marketing professionals who are pushing into this brave new world—doing what they can to build platforms for the one-screen world and working with utilitarianism marketing opportunities—the majority are lazy.

Maybe *lazy* is a bad choice of words, but a majority of marketers are simply doing everything that they have always done. The easy path. The road that was laid out for them by their predecessors. Primarily, they're relying on people who make very traditional media decisions and then execute them—uniformly— across all media platforms... because all media platforms are the same... right?

We're not talking about imploding everything. We're talking about a reboot. We're talking about thinking about things in a squiggly way. There is no doubt that certain strategies and tactics work, but it's the lazy mentality that will take you down. The truth is that most chief marketing officers don't keep their jobs for much more than twenty months (although a recent survey by executive recruitment firm Spencer Stuart places tenure at forty-three months). On top of that, most advertising agencies are dropped, changed, or sent back to re-pitch the business every eighteen months or so, but this should not be an excuse to just let the media direct how and where to spend the marketing money. Is there ROI in new media? The answer is yes (of course), but marketing professionals are asking the wrong questions and getting bad outcomes because of it.

WHAT ARE THE RIGHT QUESTIONS?

Embracing the squiggle and getting over the lazy means that you have to ask yourself the following one question: Am I willing to do the long, hard, and disruptive work so that I can create a brand ecosystem that I can measure?

You see, the tools, technology, and strategies exist—you can measure every link, image, or channel that you're thinking about engaging with. The challenge is that you need to create a formal framework that details what you're trying to accomplish, how you're going to measure it, and the economic value that it will bring. From that framework comes the even harder work of deploying it throughout the organization—getting everyone from the C-suite down to agree and to be a part of this new marketing movement toward optimization and efficacy. And if all this isn't hard enough, once you overcome those hurdles you have to actually do the work. Not just once. But constantly and consistently. You have to wake up in the morning—every day—with a smile on your face and say to yourself (and your team), "Today is a great day! We're going to reboot what doesn't work, test more things, tweak others, build newer metrics, and keep at it."

WHAT DOES THE SQUIGGLE REALLY MEAN?

Here's the truth about your career in a Ctrl Alt Delete world: It's time to stop asking others to convince us about new opportunities (because they're not all that new anymore), and it's time to start doing the hard work of getting things right. For ourselves. For the businesses that we work for. For the industry that we serve. For our legacy. Because to squiggle is the new path in a world of purgatory.

LESSONS FROM A SQUIGGLY CAREER...

Lesson #1—Don't be afraid of short and powerful projects.

We used to live in a world where human resources would look at a résumé and say, "My, this individual sure has had a lot of job switches. I wonder what the issue is?" We currently live in a world where projects and great work can get done in short periods of time. We also live in a world where a job within an organization doesn't have to be an open-ended position that just drones on and on forever. The world has changed. Don't be afraid to have many short projects as a part of your living résumé, so long as you can prove that the moves you've been making were done because you accomplished (and surpassed) the pre-established goals.

The new future of business is about putting things into market—constantly, quickly, and intelligently. If you're not constantly working to put ideas, innovations, and products into market, then what exactly are you doing? One of my business partners and CEO at Twist Image, Mark Goodman, used to have a sign hanging in his office that read: BE BRILLIANT. BE BRIEF. BE GONE. Amen.

Lesson #2—Don't be afraid of big.

Be brave. Think big. Act big. When you embrace the squiggle, it's not just about your career trajectory but about what your career can become. We now live in a world that is being changed—almost every day—because technology has become a direct part of the business and ideation (instead of simply being a part of our productivity—as it was in previous decades). Finally, we don't just have to dream up big thoughts; we must act on them, because we live in a world where big ideas can be accomplished with a lot less. As Twitter continues to grow, its creator, Jack Dorsey, went on to start Square as well. The vision statement for Square is "no more cash registers." It's more than a big, bold, and brave statement. Can you imagine a world without cash registers? Dorsey isn't just imagining it...he's tackling the big challenge. Squiggly means that you can't hide behind small thinking and quarterly employee reviews. This means that we can't be afraid to have a more squiggly career path, and we also have to be more open to doing the big, big stuff (Steve Jobs would often talk about making a "dent in the universe"). You will hear Mark Zuckerberg talk about Facebook as the place to connect the world. Sergey Brin and Larry Page of Google often talk about Google's mission to organize the world's information and knowledge (and, with that, they squiggle to create self-driving cars!). It's one thing to dream big. It's another thing to think and do big. In this new world, the squiggle is about not being afraid of the big stuff within whatever industry you serve. If you're not thinking about the bigger problems that face your industry, someone else is. Squiggle...uncover and go after the big ideas.

Lesson #3—Get squiggly.

It's not about doing what you love or being passionate about the work that you do, but about recognizing that you may be stuck or afraid to change simply because of the decisions that you made and followed back in high school and university (or because your predecessor did things a certain way). They say that you can't teach an old dog new tricks. This may be true, but you can certainly get just a little squiggly every now and then. Take on a challenge within your organization, work with a new department, change something within your business that is antiquated or draconian. Know that some of the most interesting people (the people you admire) have had very squiggly careers...and you should too.

Lesson #4—Be incompatible (maybe just a little bit).

There was a Bloomberg TV documentary titled *Bloomberg Game Changers: Steve Jobs.* There's no doubt that Jobs was an iconoclast, but what really struck me was when someone described him as "incompatible," and pushed it further by saying that's what made him so unique, special, and creative. Guy Kawasaki (a former Apple employee) went on to add that Jobs was so different from most other people that getting him to think like everybody else would be like trying to explain flying to a fish.

For your career to be squiggly, think about what it takes to really break through. Think about what it takes to be a visionary. Think about what it takes to actually change the game. It's not easy. People are not going to like you, and odds are that you're not going to be able to be exceedingly social, simply because you see things differently.

Ask yourself: What makes someone incompatible?

- **Change.** Incompatible people don't mind change at all. They try. They fail. They change. They don't look back. They look forward. The only constant in their lives is that things *will* change, and this is fine with them as long as it leads to perfection.
- **Disruptive force.** Most people see their actions as irrational. These people scream, yell, and probably demand what seems to be the impossible out of people. They don't work regular hours. They don't care much for vacation. Their work/life balance looks nothing like ours. In the end,

the people who worked for individuals like this often say that their boss helped them achieve things that they never thought they could accomplish.

- **Being an artist.** It doesn't matter if they're inventing the iPad or a new irrigation system. Their work is not their work. Their work is their *art*. It is what they were meant to do and, in the end, it is art—both in the creation process and in the final product. Incompatibles embrace the artist's way and follow their business muse. They don't care much about market research or customer insights. They know better than both (whether you like it or not).

- **Being revolutionary.** The work they do isn't just a few steps above the competition. They are—literally— revolutionizing their industry (and sometimes even creating their own industry). Everything they do is about causing maximum disruption to the way things used to be.

- **Being alone.** There are only a handful of visionaries. The word may be tossed around to describe a whole lot of business executives, but there are only a few true visionaries. These people are usually very lonely. They are lost in their ideas and drive. It makes it challenging to navigate relationships; they feel that others just don't have the knowledge base to comprehend them. Yes, they believe others are stupider than they are. The smartest of the incompatibles are able to self-diagnose and surround themselves with people who can make their visions become masterpieces.

BE A LITTLE SQUIGGLY. BE A LITTLE INCOMPATIBLE.

Being squiggly or incompatible is not a bad thing. It's easy to be negative about people who are incompatible or those who have squiggly careers, but can you imagine a world *without* people who did not fit in? One without those who knew there was a better or different way to do things? The words from Apple's infamous "Here's to the crazy ones" advertising campaign ring true...

> Here's to the crazy ones.
> The misfits.
> The rebels.
> The troublemakers.
> The round pegs in the square holes.
> The ones who see things differently.
> They're not fond of rules.
> And they have no respect for the status quo.
> You can praise them, disagree with them, quote them, disbelieve them, glorify or vilify them.
> About the only thing you can't do is ignore them.
> Because they change things.
> They invent. They imagine. They heal.
> They explore. They create. They inspire.
> They push the human race forward.
> Maybe they have to be crazy.
> How else can you stare at an empty canvas and see a work of art?
> Or sit in silence and hear a song that's never been written?
> Or gaze at a red planet and see a laboratory on wheels?
> We make tools for these kinds of people.
> While some see them as the crazy ones, we see genius.
> Because the people who are crazy enough to think they can change the world are the ones who do.

These people... *you*... are able to embrace the squiggle.

This doesn't mean that you have to suddenly change your ways. Just know and understand why these people are the way they are. It's also important to think deeply about your own definition of the word *career*. This isn't a generational issue, but one based on the reality of business as we know it today. Is there really a need for you to be sitting behind a desk—day in and day out—doing the job that you're currently doing? Or is there a way for your career to better balance your interests, attention span, and what needs to get done for some breakthrough work to come through?

Indeed, start looking at the most interesting people you know...the ones who have had true success (by your own definition) with the work that they do. The one component that the majority of them will have in common is a very squiggly career (with a dash of incompatibility). Start getting squiggly.

CHAPTER 8

The New Way We Work

New thinking for the new workplace.

In April 2010, the passengers of the Copenhagen Metro crammed onto the train's platforms for their daily commute to work. The weather was fair and clear. As they waited for the subway to arrive, many people were either buried in a book or sporting earbuds to block out the sounds of the bustling city. Mothers pushed their babies in carriages as businesspeople in suits thumbed their smartphones next to students who were doing the same thing. As the train arrived, the standard loading and unloading process began. It's not so much a mad rush or pushing as it is a collective set of shrugs, shuffles, and awkward pressings of the flesh. Some people jockeyed for a seat while others were just looking for a pole to hold on to. The majority of people stared off into the landscape in a half-awake glaze of reality.

And then something totally unexpected occurred.

The typical pinging and announcements over the loudspeaker were muted by the well-known flute intro to Grieg's *Peer Gynt* (a Danish classic). Some people thought it was pre-recorded music, while others stood by, intently watching the seated female flutist play the first phrase. Some smiled, while others tried to figure out why this woman was suddenly playing live classical music on their train. A sudden flash mob erupted as the entire Copenhagen Philharmonic (also known as Sjællands Symfoniorkester) continued to perform a full-on recital. Passengers removed their headsets and quit their idle banter to soak in the beautiful music being performed so masterfully by these passionate and dedicated musicians (some passengers shed tears of joy).

Flash mobs (groups of individuals who come together in a public venue to perform a predetermined act for a brief time and then disperse) have been happening for over a decade. They are nothing new. While they range from public pillow fights and live remakes of Michael Jackson's "Thriller" to beautiful and creative moments like this one in Copenhagen, there is something magical that happens when the planned collides with the unplanned.

Sometimes this works magically well (just ask Jay-Z and Kanye West); sometimes it doesn't seem to turn into anything interesting at all (take a listen to Pat Boone's *In a Metal Mood* album). The point is that working in silos is no longer an option because greatness comes during these moments of collision. We need divergent opinions to collide, and we need to allow space at work for everyone to not only collaborate on the bigger initiatives but create these very real and live combinations of mashups, flash mobs, and more. *It's not going to happen if you wait for the boss to tell you to make it happen.* It's only going to happen when you, as the leader of your own squiggly career, create opportunities to embrace more and more moments of collision.

COLLISIONS MAKE THE WORLD GO ROUND.

We live in a world of collisions where, for example, creative designers are paired with software engineers, and the results can be astounding (think iPad). We live in a world where marketing agencies hire anthropologists to better understand human nature, evolutionary movements, and how we all connect better to one another in the hope of making the marketing better. And yet, with all these strides toward diversifying the workforce, we still worry for our jobs because any little indiscretion gets the attention of the HR department and suddenly our file has a red flag on it. Collisions are not about breaking the rules or upsetting the applecart. The great innovative achievements of tomorrow are happening today in one place: inside these powerful moments of collision.

Unfortunately, most organizations are structured with silos or levels of hierarchy (or both) that frown upon opportunities for divergent groups to come together and to collide; indeed, these same organizations actually create infrastructure, procedures, and restrictions to keep them from happening (it's almost hard to imagine). Since you have now embraced your digital-first posture and committed yourself to a long and squiggly career road, the next step is to better understand how to make yourself more open to moments of collision, because this is where the greatness happens in the work that you do (and how you develop as a human being in these strange and fascinating times). What these initial collisions also provide are optics into how different the work that we do has become and how different it is going to be moving forward through this moment of purgatory.

Many of the emotions and values that didn't belong in the boardroom have now become central to a new business model for success. For the majority, the world of work used to mean going to work (getting there on time and leaving at around 5 p.m.— with a good hour-long lunch break and some smaller breaks in between). That has quickly changed. Today, if you're not the entrepreneur who started the business, the expectation (and your personal ambition) is that you will be an entrepreneur within it. We're expected to be tethered to our smartphones and "on call all the time."

Many cry for more work/life balance, while others embrace this as the new normal. In a globally competitive and technologically connected environment, where the next great business competitor is probably able to do a whole lot more with a whole lot less (like with two MacBook Airs and an Internet connection), the question is no longer about whether the new attitude toward work is right or wrong. Rather, it's about what we need to bring to our work—every day—to make us (and the businesses we serve) that much better.

BE THE PERPETUAL ENTREPRENEUR.

In a world where many people are looking for jobs, it's time for all of us to start thinking like entrepreneurs. In fact, be the perpetual entrepreneur whether you're writing the checks or banking them.

An entrepreneur is much more than someone with an idea who has the wherewithal (financial and otherwise) to pursue it. An entrepreneur is much more than someone with an ability to take an idea and execute it. An entrepreneur is much more than an individual who is willing and able to secure the funding and resources to make an idea happen. A true entrepreneur is someone who has an uncanny desire to create the future; someone who sees inefficiencies in the work we're doing—day in and day out. It's the stuff that you and your co-workers complain about during the lunch break. It's the stuff that you may think is unfixable. It's simply not the case. Too many people in too many places focus on everything but that critical aspect of what it takes to be an entrepreneur or an entrepreneur within . . . and it bears repeating:

An entrepreneur is someone who has an uncanny desire
to create the future.

The best business models and the companies with the most innovation all started out with an individual (or a team of people) who believed that the future success of their industry would look very different from its current state. It should come as no surprise that there is no time like the present to embrace this type of ideology. Once everything kicks into place (funding, resources, etc.) something happens . . . and this is where the wheels of innovation can slow down (or grind to a complete halt). This is the biggest challenge that faces the majority of businesses today: Most entrepreneurs eventually become business owners. They stop worrying about how to create the future and start worrying about how to grow their current revenue baseline—they strategize about how to maintain the status quo.

Business owners think a lot less about creating the future because they are much too concerned with both mitigating risk and minimizing mistakes. There's nothing wrong with being a business owner (as opposed to an entrepreneur), but it's an important distinction to make as we lurk in these moments of purgatory. The minute most entrepreneurs experience a semblance of success, their posture does change and they become a lot like business owners. Yes, there are exceptions; in fact, if we were to name them, odds are that they are also the ones we hold in the highest esteem. It's normal, it's common, but it is a tragic warning that in this day and age, being a business whose sole purpose is to mitigate risk and minimize mistakes is to be a business that will never make it through this purgatory. It's understandable in one sense, because with success comes a bigger payroll; as an entrepreneur you're now financially responsible for much more than your own rent (families now count on you to deliver). Success also breeds complacency. It's easy to keep successfully doing what works and pull a fair wage for a fair product/service out of the world. No harm, no foul. But perpetual entrepreneurship is hard. Having to think about constant invention and innovation, while sustaining growth, as your own frontier develops can be very scary. Just ask the leadership at BlackBerry, Kodak, and others.

Think about it this way: If you were a computer and software manufacturer, would you have the perpetual entrepreneurial guts to take a 180-degree turn and start producing a smartphone? What about digital music players? What about the platform to sell music? What about a touch tablet (after the failure of so many in this exact arena)?

The amazing success of the people at the heart of Apple (and many other brands that embrace perpetual entrepreneurship) comes from their ability to do much more than just be business owners with a flock of employees. It comes from their perpetual entrepreneurial spirit to innovate. And it's an innovation that is owned by every member of the team. In case you are wondering what this looks like, in May of last year, *New York Magazine* ran an article titled "The Maturation of the Billionaire Boy-Man." In it, author Henry Bloget reported that two-thirds of Apple's revenue came from products that were invented from 2007 onward. One of the most memorable lines out of Walter Isaacson's biography of Steve Jobs was this quote: "If you don't cannibalize yourself, someone else will."

The question becomes this: Is there a critical path or road map for the rest of us? Is it really possible for the rest of us to be as innovative and risk-taking as Apple? If it were possible, then Apple would not seem to be so different, brave, and bold. That being said, there are some common threads that weave through the most entrepreneurial individuals and organizations. For some this involves their ability to embrace new business models; for others it's the ability to respect the business owners that they have become, while still embracing their internal entrepreneurs (and letting that mindset roam free). Regardless, the future is not going to be established by the business owners of today. The future is going to be created by the entrepreneurs who have the vision, business mindset, and courage to not fall into the business *owner's* mindset of mitigating risk and minimizing mistakes.

When I speak to groups I often ask people to raise their hands if they are the type of people who, on any given Sunday night, can't wait for Monday morning. I'm not talking about those who are happy to get back to work because they're tired of their kids crying or having to pick the laundry off the floor. I'm talking about the people who are like wild racehorses at the gates when the horns are about to sound. They simply cannot wait to get rolling. To get up and take on that new day...those new opportunities. You won't be surprised to know how often that question incites chuckling, laughter, and the shaking of heads. If someone does raise a hand, there are typically a bunch of comments like "Quit sucking up because your boss is here," and a half-coughed "*Loser.*"

Last year, I had the pleasure of speaking to the New York City chapter of EO (Entrepreneurs' Organization). Founded in 1987 as a support group and network for entrepreneurs, the group is now a global business network consisting of eight-thousand-plus business owners with over one hundred twenty chapters in forty countries. These are people who don't want to succeed...they *have* to succeed. They are driven by a passion for success. They see being an entrepreneur not as a vocation, but as a lifelong pursuit. It is the work that they were meant to do. When I asked them that same exact question, take a guess as to how many hands were raised? Yes. The entire room. (The only exceptions were a couple of spouses in attendance. They just looked to their partners knowingly, acknowledging the people that they chose to spend the rest of their lives with.)

So who do you think the future belongs to? Those who can't

wait for Monday or those who are dreading it? Which category do you fall into? Seeking moments of collision, looking for new and interesting projects to take on, understanding that work has become a project-based place where groups come together, solve problems, and then look for more problems, have all become parts of the new normal for most businesses. It is those exact skill sets that you must embrace in the here and now.

FIND YOUR BLEND (AND FORGET ABOUT WORK/LIFE BALANCE).

In this new era of figuring out how to be great within this new way of working, I've come to believe that work/life balance as we have known it in the past is a myth. That personal truism was validated when friends from Google invited me to a private event for their chief financial officer, Patrick Pichette. Pichette was formerly a senior executive at Bell, and many of his old colleagues were also invited to this dinner. During cocktails, a former Bell colleague asked Pichette what his life was like at Google and whether or not he had a good work/life balance. I thought the question was interesting considering all of the amenities that Google provides—free gourmet food, exercise facilities, laundry service, massages, medical, and much more.

On top of the amazingly generous employee benefits program, Google also has an initiative where 20 percent of employees' time can be committed to their own pet projects. As hard as Google employees work, it seems like the company is doing everything it can to ensure that there is a healthy sense of work/life balance. Google's work environment has become legendary—the kind of work environment the rest of us are jealous of. What was Patrick's answer to this question?

"You don't take a job like this if you want balance."

His answer stopped me dead in my tracks. We would like to think that we can have it all, but it turns out that the real superstars in our world are working themselves to the bone. The difference here is that they're doing it knowingly and willingly. They take these hard assignments with a time frame and plan, preset in their minds. You could tell by Patrick's direct answer that he'd not only known what he was getting into, but accepted it as a part of what his life would become. He also seems very happy and proud of this choice. He has no plans to spend three decades in the same office and job to earn a gold watch for his service. New times, indeed.

Patrick's comment sums up the new work posture. No entrepreneur takes on initiatives to have work/life balance. Personally, I don't search for new clients, write blog posts daily, podcast, speak at events all over the world, or write articles or business books to achieve work/life balance. I do all of this (and run a hundred-plus-person marketing agency) because it's the work that I was meant to do. I'm not bragging. Just stating that what I do plays a major part in who I am. What about you? While you may read this as unhealthy, I took my opportunity to dig deeper into Patrick's comment over dinner with him. He went on to say that while he can't have any semblance of work/life balance in his type of work, he has what he calls a "healthy blend."

FIND YOUR BLEND.

What does a healthy blend look like? While Patrick is running around the world managing the finances for one of the biggest and most valuable companies anywhere, he often finds himself starting work early, working through lunch, and meeting clients in the evening. On a recent trip, he was working in Europe and invited his wife to meet him at the end of the week in London. He spent a long weekend there. This is blend...finding the opportunities to blend your life so it's not all focused on either work or play. They all blend together. I've done similar things. I was once invited to speak in Singapore and took my wife along with me; we extended the trip with a visit to Bangkok and Phuket. When I'm on a family vacation, I'll often take an hour (here and there) to quickly check emails or to catch up on some reading. Blend. In another instance, I was speaking at a major event and had some client deadlines to meet. I spoke in the morning (and knew that I had some clients to entertain in the evening), so as noon rolled around, I put the Mac-Book Air down, walked over to a movie theater, grabbed a salad to go, and took in a movie. More blend. I found the time to get the client work done and meet my deadlines after the movie.

I'm sure there are a handful of health practitioners who will shake their fingers and say that simply finding a blend is not enough; that people like Patrick and myself are headed toward burnout because we don't have a true work/life balance. I'm not sure that I would agree. The reason? I love what I do, and I don't consider it work. Whether it's answering emails, helping a client out with a business challenge, or writing this book, it's not a chore and it doesn't look, act, or feel like hard work. It's not something that I ever feel I need a break from. There is a world of difference between stress that comes from the things you want to do and the stress that comes when you feel like you're not working on the stuff that matters most to you. Hopefully, you now know in which camp you need to be pitching your own tent.

As I write these words, it's a beautiful Sunday afternoon. I'm working from my patio as my young children and wife take a nap. I woke up this morning, took the kids to an activity, then I wrote a little bit more as the kids attended a birthday party; I'll put the laptop down once they get up so we can all play in the park, then have dinner and bath time together. I love seeing life as a blend.

The most influential and powerful people I know have plenty of blend (no matter how busy their schedules look to the outside world). The most adaptive path for you to find your success in these times of purgatory will be in your ability to forget about the notion of work/life balance and find the blend in your work, personal, and community life. The squiggle of life, if you will.

MAKE YOURSELF INDISPENSABLE.

Even as certain industries and sectors claw their way back to some sort of semblance of normalcy following the recession, some of your peers are still being laid off, budgets are being slashed, and businesses are still grappling with how to do more with less. Moments of purgatory are also moments of severe confusion and uncertainty. In all of this, those individuals who are still on top of their game seem to be doing just fine. Some have even been thriving. Some have delivered new business models that changed our world forever and made people billionaires.

When the recession was in full throttle, I found myself in a conversation with one of the head talent recruiters for an exclusive fashion retail chain. As we were discussing the economy and its impact on the luxury industry, I asked how it was affecting staffing, and if it was hard to see so many people being let go from the team. When the recession was at its highest, this chain had to offer clientele brown paper bags for their purchases because many customers were embarrassed to be buying such high-end goods while people were starving in the streets. It was just that bad. This senior executive talent recruiter took a deep breath, looked me in the eyes, and said: "The top performers are doing just fine. Their jobs were never in jeopardy. They're still making lots of money and performing exceedingly well." Here's the translation: People who make themselves indispensable *are* indispensable—whether it's a time of mass economic health or whether the economy is a mess.

The challenge is in making this statement tangible. The truth behind the message is that not everyone has the strategy, tools, and tactics to get themselves to the point where they are indispensable—until now. Seth Godin was making himself indispensable long before he earned his MBA in marketing from Stanford Business School in the mid-1980s. Along with a track record that includes stints as an entrepreneur having sold one of his companies to Yahoo!, where he became vice president of direct marketing, he is also known as one of the top-rated marketing presenters on the speaking circuit and a bestselling author. From his classic *Permission Marketing* all the way to *All Marketers Are Liars*, Godin's work is rooted in simple messages that every businessperson can relate to. In January 2010, he released a book titled *Linchpin: Are You Indispensable?* This *New York Times* bestseller was all about individuals who have made themselves "linchpins"—those an organization can't be without. In his seminal book *Purple Cow: Transform Your Business by Being Remarkable*, Godin pleaded with businesses to not produce and distribute mediocre products and services. Godin describes *Linchpin* as "*Purple Cow* for people."

"There used to be a gatekeeper. A legitimate, real keeper of a real gate," Godin told me. "If you wanted to get a job at Ford, the gatekeeper needed to let you in. If you wanted to get a job at a newspaper, the gatekeeper would let you in. Either you were 'out' or you were 'in.' We organized our schools and businesses around this dichotomy of 'insiders' and 'outsiders.' I am trying to teach people that these gatekeepers are now all gone. If you want to make something in China and sell it at your local store, all you need is an email account and you're 'in.' If you want to be a blogger, all you need is a computer and you're 'in.' This means that you can be 'in' something in about a day or less. It doesn't mean that you're going to be good or successful at it, it just means that you're in it. Once we have a world like that, it raises the bar for what it means to be good, because there are so many people who are in it. There are lots of things you can do now. Go ahead and pick one...just do it."

Now more people than ever are either "in" or working for people who have realized that they are "in." It changes the dynamics of work completely. You don't need a big company that offers a solid pension to provide you with any level of security and insurance. All you need to do is to make yourself indispensable in each thing that you do. And while that may very well come off as an "easier said than done" type of platitude, Godin believes we don't have a choice anymore (and I agree with him wholeheartedly). You can't just sit back and go about your job hoping others will take you to your personal Promised Land. The evolutions of technology, connectivity, and the economy have changed everything. Individuals are using these changes to their personal advantage and growth. They are rebooting who they are.

"You don't win by being more average than other people in your industry," Godin continues. "You don't win by being more compliant than your fellow co-workers. Being more obedient at what you do every day is not going to make you more indispensable. What makes someone indispensable is that they do something that other people can't do...We go to work every day trying to not do that. We go to work trying to be just like everyone else, because that feels safe. In today's economy, and for the foreseeable future, that's the riskiest thing we can do."

Godin pushes the linchpin concept even further by encouraging individuals to explore what their "art" is (as we have already discussed). "It has nothing to do with oil paint or marble. Art is what we're doing when we do our best work." After that conversation with Godin, I not only turned my work into my art, but I began to take the work that I do very seriously (as an artist would). Some took it to mean that I was becoming pretentious. Nothing could be further from the truth. Instead of dreading Monday and the next week of work, seeing my work as art encouraged me to be challenged, excited, and ready to take on the day . . . the next project. What would your mindset be if you went to work not thinking of it as work (or your job) but as the art that you were meant to do? The work that you were meant to do? What would happen if you didn't just think of yourself as indispensable to the business's success but spent your days actually making yourself indispensable?

How does Godin look at the notion of work/life balance? "Instead of wondering when your next vacation is, maybe you set up a life you don't need to escape from," he says.

Pretty smart.

EIGHT WAYS TO SCORE A NEW GIG IN THE NEW WAY WE WORK.

The ultimate truth to finding the work that you were meant to do is not about your résumé, your experience, or how you did in the job interview (sorry). The true answer is that it is a very subjective process, which is why it is extremely frustrating to so many.

What one recruiter sees as a star, another sees as a dud. Scoring that elusive position has much more to do with the chemistry in the room than how you present your facts on an $8\frac{1}{2} \times 11$ sheet of white paper—all of which can also be very subjective from one person to another. Here are eight ways to game the system . . .

1. **Understand the process.** Too many people think that gaining their desired position is about jumping through the right

hoops: Sending in a résumé will jump you forward to an interview, which will jump you to a second interview, which will jump you through to an offer, which will jump you through to the job. This is actually the wrong process to take. The process is that you have to win the job from the second your name comes across the desk of the recruiter. Every other phase is also about one line of focus: getting the job. Don't let it go to a scorecard and don't try to just check-box your way to the next stage. You have to reframe your thinking and ask yourself, *How do I win this job from the second they see my name?*

2. **Present better.** Learn how to sell yourself better. This is never easy. There is a fine line between confidence and arrogance. There is a fine line between having an education and presenting it as experience. Learning how to present will not only be your most valuable asset when looking for that dream position, it is a skill set that will literally propel you to the C-suite. The individuals we regard as the best of the best in business all have one trait in common: They know how to present well...and with grace. Do everything you can to improve your presentation skills.

3. **Be ready before you submit a résumé.** Social media is king here. Whether it's Twitter, a blog, a podcast, or even a Facebook page, you have the ability to publish your thoughts (who you are and how you think), in text, images, audio, and video, instantly and for free to the world. If you really want to be working in this industry and you have a passion for it, you have the ability to express it. Even if it's just by sharing links you find interesting, this three-dimensional perspective will provide recruiters with a better idea about your personality and your thinking. And yes, this includes who you are connected to and how you interact with them. Whether or not it's "fair play" for a recruiter to be looking at social media

is not the point; this information is in the public domain, so shine the best light possible on yourself. And trust me, they're Googling and Facebooking you.

4. **Don't lie.** I've heard some scary stories from recruiters. I've heard that upward of 70 percent of all résumés include either lies or large embellishments. Don't lie. It's not worth it. Tell the truth and let that truth come out in your résumé, online presence, and in that first interview (should it be granted). Just ask former Yahoo! CEO Scott Thompson. The unraveling of his short tenure as head of the beleaguered digital media company happened because Thompson falsified his résumé by claiming to have had a computer science degree when he didn't.

5. **Know the industry.** There's no excuse to not know everything about the company—from the clients to the management, the competitors, the marketplace, and the industry as a whole. It used to be that you had to subscribe (and pay big money) to get that kind of information via the industry trade publications. Now, thanks to the Internet and social media, the majority of this information is online and free for you to access. It's incumbent on you to know the industry inside out. It's also important to express your constant education within the industry in everything from your initial note of contact down to the interview. You are not expected to be an expert, but it's a shame when people come in to meet our agency and they really don't know the landscape of the work that we do. It's even worse when they say things like "But I'm eager to learn!" If you're eager to learn, why haven't you been learning already?

6. **Read and write.** I didn't do well in school at all, but I didn't let my schooling get in the way of my education. If you don't have a passion for reading and writing, find one. Your success in life (forget the interview process) is dependent on it. There are no excuses. You need to know how to construct a letter

without basic spelling and grammar mistakes. Sad that I have to write that, isn't it? But it's true. You would be shocked at some of the emails and letters for work that we receive, littered with basic mistakes. Any real work that you do will be all about *communication*, so you need to be great at it. Reading is also important. You may not have that much experience, but there's no reason to not be knowledgeable.

7. **Be you.** For years, I spent my life trying to be the person that I thought everyone expected me to be in this industry. If anything was holding me back...it was that. This doesn't mean that you should be a freak (unless that's the type of position you're applying for). It does, however, mean that you really need to spend some serious time figuring out who you are and what you represent (I'm getting a little sour on the term *personal brand*, but this is what you need to be thinking about). Oscar Wilde said it best: "Be yourself; everyone else is already taken."

8. **Network.** Get out there. Go to both *free and paid* events. Connect to online events. Don't be slimy on LinkedIn, because it's a great place to network (when done right). Don't be desperate. Go there to learn, connect, and share. Don't go there looking for a job. I know it's very difficult when you're stuck or transitioning into a new career, but network for the sake of networking. Network to be helpful to others first.

LESSONS FROM THE FRONT LINES OF THE NEW WORK WORLD...

Lesson #1—Mindshift.

If you have never taken the opportunity to look at what is being done in the field of behavioral economics, you really should. A great primer on this is Dan Ariely's bestselling business book *Predictably Irrational*. What we learn by looking at behavioral economics is that human beings are very complex and irrational decision makers. Most of the bigger business decisions that are made are influenced more by our emotions and our gut than anything else. It's not as scientific as we may think—and in fact, the science behind our decisions validates a lot of this. To change our present purgatory, we are going to need to make a slight (make that major!) mindshift. We'll need to not only look at things differently, but to spend some time evaluating our true purpose and essence when layered against the work that we're doing. This mindshift means that we need to spend our days living in moments of discovery.

This discovery should push you and your thinking out to the fringes, to different places of personal experimentation with the work that you are doing. If you don't experiment and if you don't become the "tip of the spear" for your industry or cause, then you may actually start losing ground (and revenue). See yourself as an explorer, colonizer, and navigator of your own destiny.

Lesson #2—Create action.

Thinking, talking, blogging, tweeting are all fine and dandy, but at a certain point it's going to have to be about action. You're going to have to push yourself to actually do the things everyone else is either just talking about or simply armchair-quarterbacking. Blogs, Facebook, and YouTube highlight this distraction from getting the work done in a twenty-four-hour new media news cycle. With tons of information readily available, there is still a significantly low percentage of people who actually do things versus those who are talking and criticizing. It's easy to be a slacktivist and it's hard to be an activist.

Lesson #3—Create provocations.

We only really discover something new when we're being provocative. This doesn't mean that you should be loud, rude, offensive, or disturbing to others; it means that you should act critically. It's about how you both think and publish your thoughts. Look at what Arianna Huffington did with the *Huffington Post*. It was (and still is) a provocative move—in both the language used within the community and the platform on which it resides. The *Huffington Post* is—for all its charms—a provocation to traditional print media and the press. In the same breath, Arianna (as a persona) is a provocation to journalism. This is why heads turned in 2012 when the *Huffington Post* was the first commercially run, U.S.-based digital media company to win a coveted Pulitzer Prize. Then, just a few months after this watershed moment for new media, Huffington and her team launched a mobile application called GPS for the Soul—a place to measure your level of stress and the tools to help you both calm yourself down and find a better center of self-peace. Is it not provocative that a company widely known as a publisher of political and op-ed pieces is suddenly publishing a stress-relieving mobile app?

Lesson #4—Play.

We often forget to have fun while doing all of this. We often think that "play" exists only as a break from "work." Let's agree that even saying, "There's work and then there's play," is probably not the best way to figure out how to fix the current situation and push your career further.

Play is direly missing from work, because way too many people are doing jobs that they hate. This is not a battle cry to up and quit your day job. This is a battle cry to inject play (and what it means) into everything that you do with your work, so that the net result allows your playfulness and excitement to ignite your co-workers and clients. The most creative and inventive people spend a lot of time playing. Warren Buffett spends the majority of his time reading. Ask Buffett if he considers this to be tedious work or if he derives great pleasure from it.

If you're worried about asking the people you work with if they would be open to more play, feel free to use the word *tinker*. When working to solve a business challenge, always ask yourself if there is still some tinkering that can be done. One easy way to add play and tinkering to your work diet is to do it either first thing in the morning or right before going to bed. There is something about those moments right before and after sleep that access some dynamic parts of the brain. Try it.

NEW ATTITUDE. NEW CAREER PATH. NEW YOU.

The skills just mentioned are soft ones. Many great books, articles, and blog posts have been written (in much more detail) about how to dig a little deeper into them, but here's another truth: You have to find, nurture, and work (very hard) at them...on your own. Only you can go to work tomorrow and foster a culture of collisions, a place where diverse people, working on different components, can come together, share, and hopefully uncover new and innovative ways for your business to grow. Your very future depends on it. Only you can decide that regardless of your lot in life, you will go to work and be the perpetual entrepreneur, constantly looking for new and innovative ways to keep your business and company at the leading edge of your industry. Only you can leverage technology to make you that much more connected not only to your consumers, but also to your peers (the ones at your physical location and the ones who work remotely). Only you can decide to cannibalize the work that you're doing before your competitors do.

With all of that complexity and new ways of thinking at work, it's infinitely important to find your blend.

There is no truer definition of a success than someone who has mastered the fine blend of work, family, friends, and community service. By attacking every day like this, you will make yourself indispensable. You will become one of those people who are untouchable, and you will be in a position to guide your own destiny rather than leaving your fate up to a spreadsheet and a bad quarter that make you prey to a company-wide downsizing strategy. And in the end, only you can find yourself not working, but rather creating art—the true manifestation of the work that you were meant to do. Take this time to celebrate the fact that while we're in this moment of purgatory, we've never before—in the history of business—had an opportunity like this to create a more fulfilling life.

CHAPTER 9

The Marketing of You

How rapid and consistent communication through powerful content is the new advertising.

A HAILSTORM OF NEW MARKETING OPPORTUNITIES.

The last two weeks of May 2012 were strange. Leading up to Monday, May 21, the world watched—with bated breath—as Facebook became a public company in what was heralded as one of the biggest initial public offerings in the history of the world. The excitement resembled the hype, pomp, and circumstance we more commonly associate with the announcement of a new world tour by U2. But in its first day of public trading, Facebook's stock didn't pop or rock or roll. It just kind of fizzled. From that moment on, the business world started pointing fingers, and the typical online banter ensued. People were suddenly very quick to throw Facebook under the bus—from investors to those who had been ardent fans of the online channel. Journalists and bloggers started calling this moment the beginning of the end for online social networking (Bubble 2.0, and so on . . .), while others called this the end of Facebook. Comparisons between Facebook's IPO and Google's (which happened in 2004) were also made, and subsequent news articles focused on Facebook's advertising and its inability to drive as much value as the advertising that was taking place on other spaces (like Google).

This is not a story about Facebook...or Google.
It's a story about you.

This massive shift in how people use and interact with media is bigger than just wondering whether media is passive or active. Brands need to play in that sphere, but the Facebook IPO disappointment highlights another fascinating trend: What we do, as individuals, to communicate, share, and build our personal profiles adds layers and dynamics to the world of marketing and how we run our collective businesses.

Think about it this way: Who are you when you are engaged in a channel like Facebook? What is your mindset? What are you doing? While Facebook loves to trot out the one-billion-plus users, it's important to note that the average user only has about 120 connections. So, while Facebook cumulatively is massive, it's really millions of very little connections that are primarily there to share personal and social information. Are such users ready to engage with a small little banner box in the same fashion that they would on a news site or a blog page? Doubtful. Are those users interested in liking a brand page and having the brand's promotions and coupons pop up in their personal news feed? The future of better marketing is your ability (and the business that you represent) to not only be real, human, and sincere, but to connect—in a very direct way—to the point where what you're publishing has enough value to be included in that 120-person social graph. It's not easy, but it's also not impossible. This is why Facebook is banking on sponsored stories and other new marketing initiatives, and it's a lesson that all of us should be paying direct attention to.

The role of the advertiser, the marketer, and you is to make that little box of advertising (or that sponsored story or direct relationship) as compelling to users as the social content that they're really there for. In short: That's a tall and hard order to deliver. Why? Because we suddenly can't lump everything together and say, "Facebook advertising does this, so Google advertising must do that." When you're on Facebook, you're connected and sharing much more personal information with a smaller group of personal connections. Few (if any) of the people we know hop onto Facebook and say, "Hey, I wonder what Target has on sale this week?" Compare that with Google. Why do you go to Google? You have intent. You are looking for something. It could be a hotel for your next vacation, an app for your smartphone, organic dog food, a great place to take your kids for a weekend getaway, a coupon for an event, and on and on.

When you're on Google, you are—more likely than not—looking for an answer to a burning question. So if a contextual ad comes up and it's relevant to your search, your inclination to click on it is much higher. This is nothing new. This is the advertising model that Google has been trumpeting and succeeding with for over a decade. What we can pull out of this very real example is that *you are not the same person when you're on Facebook as you are when you're on Google*. How you communicate and connect must be fundamentally different in a world where more and more people are connected through these digital channels and are sharing at such a dramatic rate.

As we have read in previous chapters, active media has many layers of depth when you compare it with passive media (which features—for the most part—a consumption mindset). You can add practically any other type of new media channel or platform into the equation (Pinterest, YouTube, whatever) and you'll note that the consumer intent in each of these spaces is radically and fundamentally different. On YouTube you're watching, sharing, and commenting on video content, which is very different from when you are on Pinterest, sharing content from other sources, putting it together around a theme, and then connecting to other like-minded individuals.

The point is this: You—as an individual—now have unprecedented numbers of spaces to create and share who you are and how you think. Beyond that, you now have unprecedented numbers of spaces to connect to like-minded people. In short, we're moving ever so quickly away from an advertising world into a world where content and context blend to become both king and queen when it comes to making your business ideas spread. There are many more niche and small spaces that each require their own strategic, creative, and innovative tinkering attitude to uncover the kernels of success. It's not so obvious.

Finding gold in the marketing of you.

From a personal standpoint, you don't need ten million likes on Facebook or fifteen million views on YouTube for these channels to be effective in helping you push through online purgatory to the Promised Land. In fact, understanding the intent of the people you are connected to and how to best add value to their experience is at the core. The sad truth is that most people don't understand the value and opportunities that come from being able to present yourself in the best possible light, from the boardroom and meetings that you attend to the online world and beyond. Most people still see these new channels as a place to beat their own chests or simply broadcast messaging (in a spammy kind of way).

Here's what it all comes down to: Great communication will lead you and your team to a place where deeper collaboration and concurrent innovation start happening—simply by rebooting how everyone communicates and defines the value of content...

starting with you...starting now. So how do you best present, market, and communicate who you are and what you offer in this evolving business world?

NOTHING HAPPENS WITHOUT KNOWING HOW TO PITCH AN IDEA.

How many days have you sat around, stomach twisted, waiting to hear if you had won a new piece of business that you pitched for? Or if you got that raise, or if a job offer came in? It's a terrible feeling, and the only thing that can alleviate it is getting the proverbial thumbs-up from the prospective client, employer, or boss. The sad truth is that it doesn't always work out in our favor. "You win some, you lose some" is the common mope you'll overhear business development professionals bellowing at the bar, while they nurse an extra-dry martini at the end of the day. Pitching, selling, and winning more business are among the most complex pieces of the business puzzle.

As a digital marketing agency, my company, Twist Image, dukes it out weekly with our competitors for the opportunity to work with a brand and handle all of their digital marketing initiatives. It is ultimately a creative (although highly strategic and technical) product that we deliver, and this complicates the business development process because—as with anything creative—the reasons we frequently win business (and sometimes lose) are very subjective. One client will think our pitch cleared the clouds and made cherry blossoms bloom, while another may think that we missed the mark.

No one knows these sides of the business better than Peter Coughter. For over twenty years, Coughter was president of Siddall, Matus & Coughter Inc., one of the most respected advertising and communications agencies in the southeast. His agency won industry awards and recognition from places like the American Marketing Association, One Show, the Clio Awards, Communications Arts, and many others. Today he is a professor at Virginia Commonwealth University's Brandcenter, and to support his teaching habit he spends a significant amount of time on the road teaching organizations—from all walks of life—how to sell their ideas better. In 2012, Coughter released his first business book, *The Art of the Pitch: Persuasion and Presentation Skills That Win Business*. In this book, Coughter deconstructs some of the most commonly held beliefs about how business is won, and what he uncovers is enlightening, entertaining, and full of lessons no business leader should be without.

Why is there an industry-wide sentiment that clients always kill the best ideas? You can transpose that line to be: Why don't people read my blog? Why didn't people like my idea in the brainstorming meeting? Why didn't I get that promotion I asked for? Coughter takes this perspective and turns it on its head in his book. It's not that great ideas got killed by the client... it's that agencies killed their own great ideas by not presenting them well.

"People pitching ideas think they're doing it in a way that the client wants to see. It's simply not true," says Coughter. "The truth of the matter is that you have to have the guts to do it the right way... which is the way that you really believe the idea must be delivered. After five minutes of watching some of my clients first present to me, I often stop them and ask if they would have enjoyed sitting through what just happened. They invariably say, 'No.' What we have to do is understand that the clients don't really know our business. They make the shoes, we make the ads. So, let's help them sell more shoes by making terrific ads. We need to sell the idea of it before we sell whatever it is that we're selling. I call it framing. We need to frame the conversation so that we eliminate all of the possible solutions, until the only solution possible is ours. When a business learns how to do this, they will markedly increase their win rate."

Conventional wisdom will garner conventional results. This is the bane of most business presentations and the presenters who give them. They don't treat the pitch as a unique moment in time to give the potential client pause. Pushing it further, they rarely take that opportunity to help the prospect fall back in love with the business they're in. "What I suggest is that we defy convention and try to create the exceptional," continues Coughter. "The reason we are in the room is to win the business. We're not there to sell a campaign or have people from within our organization demonstrate how intelligent they are. We observe convention and plug people into holes to fill the room and look big. There was one instance, early in my career, where we defied convention. We decided that I, alone, would present to the client. That's what we did. I did an hour and a half alone with just some videos and creative work to show. I left the stage after my pitch, looked out into the seats and saw that people were crying. When you can make them cry, you win," he laughs.

The challenge is that most presentations, blog posts, Facebook pages, and YouTube videos make people cry, but for an entirely different reason. They cry because they are bored. They cry because they feel that they wasted their time. We all pitch business. We all want to win more business. We all spend our time trying to pitch something in social media (an idea, a thought, a message). We are constantly in "pitch mode," yet so few people think about how to get better and better at pitching their ideas—from the boardroom to their Facebook timeline.

Life's a pitch. Deal with it.

If social media has shown us anything, it's that we are all—constantly—pitching ourselves. Some may see this as narcissistic, while others may call it pathetic, but the truth is that we are all promoting ourselves, oversharing, and connecting like never before. If the marketing imperative is strictly to interrupt those who are doing this, there is a missed opportunity. The way in which we move away from a world of narcissism into a space of value is in realizing that with so many interested and connected individuals online, the true opportunity is to take a step back from all of the self-promoting chest thumping and to dig down deep and uncover and connect with those who can offer a mutually beneficial connection. Yes, there will always be the scammers and the spammers, but we're entering an interesting era in which pitching and self-promoting become more real, human, and sincere. The problem is that businesses are constantly looking to game the system, to cheat, to take the humanness out of it. Don't automate your sincerity and your connections.

SOCIAL MEDIA AUTOMATION, RESPECT, CREDIBILITY, AND ROBOTS.

An online service was introduced a few years back that enabled people on Twitter to bring together a small group of trusted bloggers that would automatically retweet out to everyone's network all of the blog posts that the group of bloggers created individually. On the surface, it seemed like an interesting idea to maximize sharing and visibility. As a blogger, you could choose the bloggers that you know and trust; all of the content created by this collective would be shared within the entire collective's Twitter network. The spirit of this platform sounds great: ensure that great content gets shared and gets attention.

But don't be a robot. Whether you're pitching or presenting ideas or looking for newer ways to connect your ideas to others, do your best to keep it as real and as human as possible. Here's my personal philosophy: I don't want to automate my tweets—even ones about blog posts from people I know, like, respect, and follow. The truth is, I don't get a chance to read everyone's blog posts all the time, and it seems disingenuous to recommend something automatically to my connections without spending some quality time with a piece of content and thinking about whether it would add real value to the people I am connected to.

Personally, it seems like automating this process (or many other online channels that allow me to pitch who I am to the rest of the world) is a little spammy; it feels wrong to recommend something that I may not have seen at all. Now, I understand that it's easy for me to write this because I have a decent-sized network already. But I'm sure those who are just developing their following are eager for a place to pitch what they're thinking to more and more people. In short, how do you build an audience? Well, if I only had a handful of followers on Twitter, I would probably be even less interested in this automated service or any other. If I only have a few people who trust me enough to follow me and connect with me, how would I ever be able to build up a network of trust and credibility if I were automating this process for such a small, close-knit community?

So can automation ever work for you? Yes, the concept works and can scale if each person within the network truly does read and follow every blog post that every blogger within the network posts, and feels that every piece of content is always worthy of sharing with their audience. Does that sound reasonable? My years of experience blogging (over a decade and growing) say no. People are inundated with content, and a place like Twitter adds a more human (and real) way to curate and edit content. If everyone winds up automating that process to tweet out every piece of content like robots, Twitter becomes nothing more than another RSS reader where your connections are choosing your subscriptions (instead of you).

I follow people on Twitter because they act as amazing curators. They're not retweeting out every blog post from the people they respect, but rather they are retweeting the best blog posts from the people they respect. You can see how this links directly with how you pitch yourself and your wares: It's about the humanness of it all. Gaining true credibility and trust online is not about automating the process. It's the same reason big brands struggle to make credible connections. And that blogger-promotion service? Triberr has since removed the automation function and has moved toward a much more personal approach based on an individual's scrutiny of selections and the promotion of bloggers within groups. So far, that level of personalization seems to work more effectively than the previous version where each individual simply blasted out links to a peer group.

THE EASIEST WAY TO GET BETTER?
DON'T BE A SOCIAL MEDIA JERK.

As you are no doubt aware, there is a plethora of information online from various personalities about what you should and should not be doing when it comes to promoting yourself and your business using social media. I've become a big believer in doing what works best for you and ignoring what most of the digerati think. Still, there are some pretty obvious faux pas that take place online. For the most part, I believe this happens because individuals feel like there are fewer ramifications if they're hiding behind a keyboard or a smartphone or an iPad than if they were standing face-to-face with you.

Always be face-to-face with the moment of connectivity. The easiest way to improve the on-ramp success of your digital efforts to build reputation is to always imagine that the person you're connecting with is standing right there in front of you. Think about it this way: *If that person were standing there—right in front of your face—would you . . .*

- **Cover your face?** Imagine speaking to someone but they kept their identity unknown. How awkward would that be? Show your face . . . post a real (and recent) photo of yourself.
- **Use a fake name?** Do you think that you're going to build trust with someone if the other person is using a nickname, fake name, or the name of the company they work for? Imagine someone asking, "What's your name?" and the response is, "My name is Scott's Plumbing!"
- **Give your business card to everyone?** Does anyone like the person at the local chamber of commerce event who runs around the room throwing out business cards as if they were ninja stars? It's not important to connect to as many people as possible in one shot . . . it's much more important to connect to the right people by taking your time and really getting to know people.
- **Be so pushy?** Someone recently asked me to connect on LinkedIn. The second that I accepted the request, I was immediately emailed a very long sales pitch about what he sells and how I could buy it. On top of that, the email included a two-meg PDF brochure attachment. This is the in-person equivalent of walking up to someone, introducing yourself, and then rambling through a twenty-minute sales presentation without their permission . . . and pickpocketing them at the same time.
- **Call them out in public?** I see this a lot on Twitter. People are loosely connected, and then one person calls the merits of the other individual's online activities out in public. Can you imagine being in a small circle of people you just

met (or sort of know) at an event, when someone turns to the entire group and says, "You see this person standing in front of you? I heard her speak before the event and I think she's completely ridiculous." That would never happen in person . . . so why do it online?

- **Ask them to do something for you without really knowing them?** The next time you're at an event, turn to the person you just met and ask if they would mind writing a reference letter for you. How would that work out for you? I'm amazed at how quickly individuals will ask for something of value (for themselves) from someone they do not know without giving value first. There's nothing wrong with asking for help, but you'll always see a more positive result if you start by delivering value first—by being valuable to others before asking them for favors. Give abundantly and be helpful.

Do your best. Be your best.

My way of building a professional network may be different from yours. You may find value in creating a process that will automate your content sharing and how you add individuals to your network. If it works for you, please feel free to toss my ideas by the wayside. The truth is that there are many individuals who have a much bigger and broader profile than I do in online and offline channels, but I would guess that there are probably very few who have the same level of substantive depth to their relationships. Why? We have to remember that receiving a follow, friend, like, +1, or the like is nothing more than someone shaking your hand in an airport. It's nothing more than a digital version of an autograph. There is nothing more or less attached to the relationship than that. Where you, as an individual, take that handshake (or digital autograph) is up to you. The true value that comes from making yourself a known entity in your industry will be predicated by your ability to pitch your ideas and connect them to people who genuinely want to get to know you better, on a continual basis, instead of simply following you and then just spamming you. My technique is to constantly and consistently deliver value in the content that I publish on my blog, in my Twitter feed, or on my Facebook timeline. You will have to find your own path.

MAKING SENSE OF THE MESS.

Ultimately, the main role of marketing yourself and being able to pitch yourself in a more compelling way is to build influence and credibility. Still, right now there are both individuals and massive corporations chasing likes, fans, and friends. Within this mad rush for likes, it's important to reflect on the fact that having millions of followers does not mean that you have any level of influence. Just because a brand or an individual is good at getting a lot of people to click a button to follow them does not mean that those people who have clicked will do everything (or anything) that you ask of them.

This was a mass-media lie that was perpetuated by the original marketing and advertising executives as a way to strong-arm brands into coughing up their dollars to line the pockets of the advertisers and media companies. It's a business that worked well until the proper analytics and platforms were put in place (thank you, technology...and yes, thank you, social media) for us to see—in living color—a semblance of a truth. The truth is new. The truth will change.

Howard Stern has millions of listeners tuning in daily to his satellite radio show and millions of people watching him as a judge on *America's Got Talent*. Charlie Sheen had millions of followers on Twitter (until he recently deleted his account) and he's bravely staging his television sitcom comeback with *Anger Management*. Yet Howard Stern has tremendous influence over his audience, while Charlie Sheen does not. (Sorry, Charlie.) Radio is not more influential than Twitter. It's all about individuals, their message, and their ability to connect it with a caring audience. Nothing more. Nothing less. Is it at all surprising that Sheen decided to quit Twitter in 2012? If you can't influence, what is the point?

Just because Howard Stern has fewer followers than Charlie Sheen on Twitter doesn't mean he is less influential. (Stern has over 1.5 million followers as of this writing, compared with Sheen who had over 7.5 million.) My guess is that if Stern asked his followers to actively do something, the conversion rate percentage would trump Sheen's request by a large multiple. Furthermore, if someone with a small following sends out a tweet with a call to action that doesn't convert, we should not assume that this individual has little influence. It simply means that this message didn't resonate with that audience at that particular moment in time. Remember, for every Arab Spring, there are thousands of movements that never take hold or that fizzle out.

The brands and individuals that are experiencing "true influence" (and I'm using quote marks here on purpose because there is no agreed-upon definition for "true influence"—this is my own personal interpretation) are doing so because they are connected to people who are having real interactions with other real human beings (and those interactions are truly meaningful). While there are a handful of brands that have influence over and above that (Apple, Starbucks, and the like), it is much more practical and realistic for businesses to think about using these opportunities to connect and have sincere engagements instead of trying to rack up cumulative numbers.

A brand's or an individual's ability to put a message in front of millions of people begins and ends with that impression. No influence comes from it alone. We (as a public) seem to believe that the influence comes from the sheer volume of impressions and connections that we have in the marketplace: that we can have influence if we beat a message into people's heads through massive repetition. But we can't. True influence comes from connecting to individuals, nurturing those relationships, adding real value to other people's lives, and doing anything and everything to serve them, so that when the time comes for you to make a request, there is someone there to lend a hand.

Worry less about how many people you are connected to, and worry a whole lot more about who you are connected to—who they are and what you are doing to value and honor them (in their spaces). It would also serve us well not to confuse an advertising campaign with a marketing strategy around building influence and engagement. They are not one and the same. Perhaps we need to stop using traditional metrics based on the movement of masses and start looking at newer analytic models. Perhaps then we can more clearly define key concepts like *influence* and *engagement*.

INFLUENCE AND CREDIBILITY THROUGH BETTER STORYTELLING.

In this world where anybody can (and does) publish content in text, images, audio, and video instantly for the entire world to see, we have to start asking ourselves this very difficult question: At what point will the proverbial levee break?

Marketers are busy telling their clients to start producing content or suffer the wrath of becoming irrelevant. Confession: My head is bowed down in shame for I am, without question, one of those marketers. Content needs to be created for a captive audience, and we may very well be selling a bill of goods here. We're asking a lot of individuals. We're telling people to create content. Short content (be on Twitter!) and long content (blog! and blog often!). We're telling brands to make videos (post them on YouTube and Vimeo and they don't have to only be sixty seconds long!), and we're telling brands to start their own radio shows (podcasting—still a massive opportunity for brands!).

Let's back up. What is the point of advertising? Advertising's function is to create awareness. Consumers need to know when a new type of toilet paper is on the market. If we trusted that they'd look at every product on the toilet paper shelves on every visit to their local merchant, we wouldn't have to advertise. But that doesn't happen. As such, we need to make our message stand out and have its own unique space. This new type of toilet paper must be distinctly unique from other toilet paper. Beyond that, is there any additional information to share? Is it the toilet paper company's fault that other brands, products, and services have also all come to the realization that they need to capture your attention—if only for a brief moment—to inform you that they exist?

Do you need a Facebook page for this? Do you need a mobile app for that? Content is a great way to create awareness as well, but this type of awareness needs a special kind of meaning and depth. Why? Because the same consumers that are inundated with advertising are also being inundated with content. That's a lot of messaging.

Also, in a world where a brand is now curating content, publishing content, and serving as a media entity unto itself (check out Red Bull Media), it's critical that we—the business leaders during this moment of purgatory—take one step back and ask ourselves: Are we asking too much of our consumers? Beyond that, are we asking even more of those who aren't even our consumers yet? This is what happens in a world where anyone can publish their thoughts in text, images, audio, and video instantly. It becomes a game where brands are jumping in the pool simply because every other brand is jumping in the pool.

What does that get you? Mediocrity at best, but junk is the more likely outcome. Prior to the social web, how many advertorials did you read that were so captivating, you could not help but rip them out of the magazine (or newspaper) and share them with friends and colleagues? Admit it—it's not easy to recall a scenario like that. There are so few companies that will admit that the quality of their content can't match the quantity that they are producing. Have you ever walked to the back of a conference hall and seen the bags and dumpsters of corporate white papers, testimonials, and articles that are left shortly after the trade show floor shuts down? You can blame bringing too many copies along as one excuse, but the sad reality is that the content just didn't captivate the audience.

So what do we do? We kill the content. You heard me: *Kill the content*.

Step away from the publish button and take a breather. Instead of looking at your content calendar or barking at someone in your organization to tweet more frequently, take a fifteen-minute siesta and ask yourself this one question: What great stories can we tell? Stop thinking about content as the endgame and consider that the true value is the stories you tell.

You can condemn a company like Apple for not being all that social, but you can't deny that their brand and products tell a wonderful story. The same is true for other brands we highlight as success stories. Zappos tells us great stories about creating happiness. Red Bull makes us believe that human beings can do impossible things. Disney creates worlds of wonder and delight for children of all ages. And, as you can see by the current state of these brands, it's not always easy to stay relevant and compelling to your audience.

Marketers will often say that the best ads are the ones that tell stories. While you can easily shoot back with a "Duh, tell me something I don't know," take a cold hard look at all of your marketing collateral and ask yourself if you're telling a story worthy of being told—or are you telling a story just to get something sold? Personally, I think that brands and content and great stories are only beginning to get good. Now, because they have the tools, channels, and distribution platforms, real magic can happen (and you don't even need to buy ad space to let the world know). What's my hope? That brands start reinvesting in great stories instead of investing in people to simply blog, tweet, and update their Facebook page.

It's not all about content. It's all about stories. It's not all about stories. It's all about *great* stories. It's a tall order, but if you're looking to create a true mark and to get people to remark about everything that you're doing, you only have one major mission when it comes to marketing yourself and the business that you represent: Go out there and create some great stories. Please.

SIX WAYS TO GET YOURSELF MORE DIGITAL AND IN TOUCH WITH THE NEW MARKETING OF YOU.

How does a business professional bridge the gap from the traditional marketing channels to where we're at now? Try these six new approaches:

1. **Learn it.** Education used to be expensive. Fortunately, it isn't for digital marketing. If you don't know where to begin, try any one of the top marketing blogs over at the *Advertising Age* Power 150 list. You can also check out the type of people I follow on Twitter. There are many smart podcasts that regularly focus on the topic of marketing (*The BeanCast, Marketing Over*

Coffee, Jaffe Juice, and *For Immediate Release* come to mind), and they're all free. Just head over to iTunes, go to the podcast section, and look for the marketing podcasts (audio and video).

2. **Read more.** It's not just about reading blogs and following people on Twitter. Get in the habit of reading...often...all the time. There are a lot of brilliant business books by people like Don Tapscott, Seth Godin, Clay Shirky, Joseph Jaffe, Avinash Kaushik, Bryan Eisenberg, Nilofer Merchant, David Weinberger, and many others that can get you started. It's amazing to think that for less than two hundred dollars you can buy the most cutting-edge thinking. Most of these books offer the kind of content that they don't teach in universities.

3. **Create more.** One of the things that makes digital marketing so fascinating is the possibility for anybody and everybody to create content as well. It's critical that you spend some of your time formulating your thoughts and publishing them online. It's not about creating an online résumé or becoming famous. It's about critical thinking and gaining a better understanding of what it means to make your thoughts sharable and findable. The act of creating in these channels will give you a better understanding of how they can connect you.

4. **Love it.** *Passion* is an overused term. But it also happens to be the right term. You have to love this stuff. For me, I can't imagine doing anything else. I get hundreds of email newsletters, Google Alerts, blog postings, and tweets about all things digital marketing and new media. When do I find the time to consume all of it? I don't. But I try to get the highlights and dig in deeper when I can.

5. **Live it.** Please go back and read the first part of chapter 6 and Avinash Kaushik's response to the marketing professional about the power of these new channels. It bears repeating:

"The Web has been around forever and yet it is not in the blood of the executives who staff the top echelons of companies. Make no mistake about it, they are smart, they are successful, and they want to do better, but the Web is such a paradigm shift that if it is not in your blood, it is very difficult to imagine its power and how to use it for good. How do you demand innovation, creativity, and radical rethink if you can't even imagine it?" You have to live it. It has to be in your blood.

6. **Practice it.** Try different things. Think about your marketing strategy: How does it connect to the other pieces of your branding and marketing strategy? What can you do today to make your consumers' experience better through these connected channels? As you dig deeper, you'll find many people talking up a good game. While what they say may be impressive, dig deeper and try to find the people who have their hands dirty. The ones who are neck-deep in these channels and platforms are the real workers and the real people worth being connected to.

LESSONS FROM THE MARKETING OF YOU...

Lesson #1—Intent is everything.

Before thinking about marketing yourself on a specific channel or platform, take a long, hard look at the channels and ask yourself this very simple question: Why are people here? What are they doing here? What is their experiential intent when they come here, and how would I—as a brand or a company—be able to better connect without disrupting their experience? Can I provide a truly additive dose of value? While looking at this level of intent, try to define a healthy sense of frequency and consistency.

What do these people like, share, and connect with most? This simple act will put consumers first in everything that you do and make all the stories that you would like to share that much more valuable to them. On the other hand, trying to force people on Facebook to do what you'd like them to do will be an act of futility, frustration, and failure.

Lesson #2—Marketing yourself should not be spammy.

Individuals and the companies that they represent have a burning urge to get people to buy from them. There is a classic sales adage that goes like this: "All things being equal, people buy from those they know, like, and trust." Jeffrey Gitomer (famed sales trainer and author of countless bestselling books on sales, such as *The Sales Bible* and *The Little Red Book of Selling*) often adds to that infamous quote by saying: "All things being unequal, people *still* buy from those they know, like, and trust."

Lesson #3—Pitch to win.

Being likable and being yourself are the keys to winning every pitch. We are all constantly pitching. We're pitching people to follow us on Twitter, or we're pitching people when we post to their Facebook walls. In my industry, I've seen countless agencies win a pitch by showing what they thought the client wanted. While they won the business, they quickly lost it because the relationship never flourished. They cheated by not being themselves during the pitch. They cheated by creating a perception instead of showing what the reality of working together could be. Pitch to win by being yourself and clearly defining your values and your creativity. Nobody likes a bait-and-switch scenario.

Lesson #4—Automation is still for robots.

You will find countless opportunities to game the system or automate something. Think about the shifting landscape of business and consumers' rabid desire to have real connections with real human beings. Instead of fighting it or trying to shy away from it, consider embracing it. These interactions lead to bigger and better business opportunities. Why not think of new and exciting ways to add more human interactions to your business instead of tools for automation?

Lesson #5—Focus on influence.

Don't languish over how many people are following or connecting to you. Spend your time connecting your business to *influence*...not reach.

Those who command true influence quickly discover that tremendous reach becomes a strategic and powerful by-product of influence. But those who influence a few can easily get those few to share and become evangelists. While your competitors are engaging in a strange arms race to grab as many friends and followers as possible, focus your time, energy, and attention on a select few where you can foster influence. You will see your reach begin to outpace those competitors, but—more important—you will have the ability to actually get others to take action.

Lesson #6—Kill your content.

If you have an editorial calendar or if you're creating content on your own, give yourself a pause. Take a break. Step back and look at the list of what you're about to publish and ask yourself if these are stories—real stories—that the people who read them will actually care about. Does your content tell a real story or is it simply a glorified press release or sales pitch? In a world where everything can be content, the winners of tomorrow will not be those who are creating and publishing content, but rather those who are telling fascinating stories and getting them shared. There's a world of difference between the two.

WHERE DO YOU GO FROM HERE?

We've come a long and far way from the early days of using Twitter or a blog to build a personal brand. In fact, the world has changed dramatically because all of us are publishing our lives via smartphone to places like Facebook, Twitter, tumblr, Path, Instagram, Google+, YouTube, Pinterest, and many more. These smaller, bite-size nuggets of our lives cumulatively tell a very personal story. Brands still think that simply interrupting these experiences with their content (not stories) is the future. It is not. Think about how your fellow human beings are connecting—at work, at home, and beyond—and start thinking about what you can do to be a better and more interesting part of this storytelling. All of this continual growth still provides us with an amazing opportunity to create limitless connections, so long as you take the time to get it right and make it right.

CHAPTER 10

Work the Space

Anywhere is your workplace.

ACE IS THE SPACE.

There's something about the business pace of New York City that no other city in the world can replicate. In mid-April of last year, I was invited to speak at a Google event there. When I'm in Manhattan, I like to walk the city as much as possible. If there was ever a way to ignite an entrepreneurial spirit within an individual, it's simply by walking the busy streets. It becomes a rap song parody: Everyone is hustling. Not only that, but those who are stuck in the lower rungs still posture like they're big-time players. I'll often find myself looking at the skyline, then down the massive buildings to the street level, as businesspeople—from all walks of life—push and power-walk while talking loudly on their mobile devices. I wonder if this is some kind of human anthill, and that I'm the only one who feels like it is.

This was a cloudy April day. Not quite summer, and thankfully not winter. As I made my way west on 29th from Park Avenue, I was reminded of a feature in *Fast Company* magazine about the Ace Hotel. Within a couple of minutes I had arrived and could not resist stepping into what many consider to be the future of the work space.

The lobby of the Ace Hotel is hard to describe. It's a combination of hipster cool, library chic, and Paris bistro flair. The long desks are somewhat off-putting at first. You wind up wondering why the lobby space for a hip hotel looks so much like a library. In traditional hotels, you would be hard-pressed to find any semblance of an electrical outlet (the truth is that those plugs are hard to find at libraries as well). Pick any hotel in any city around the globe and you can usually spot the businesspeople with their about-to-die BlackBerrys as they're hunched over in a corner, half covered by a drape and on their hands and knees trying to plug their smartphone into the coffee table without knocking the expensive lamp over. Not at the Ace Hotel. Not only do these long library desks consume the entire center of the main lobby, but next to each seat is a power plug, and you can tell that these desks were customized for people who need to be plugged in all day.

In short, Ace Hotel has turned a regular hotel lobby into a communal work space. Nobody is there trying to shuttle you to a room and there is no hustling from the wait staff to buy drinks or food. People come to the hotel (the majority of them are not guests, but native New Yorkers) to plug in, connect to the Internet, and run their businesses. This is one hotel that is encouraging people to come, squat, and work.

And it's cool. You can feel the energy. This is what Richard Florida was describing in 2004 when he released his bestselling book *The Rise of the Creative Class*. Creativity in our economy has not only become one of the key growth areas (as Florida predicted), but it is increasingly becoming the core unique selling proposition to everything. The challenge with creativity is that it does not align with how our work spaces have been planned and urbanized to date. On top of that, our traditional work spaces are slowly adapting to technology but have yet to fully embrace the many new ways that most of us work with technology to make things better, faster, and smarter. (How many of us still work for companies that block Internet access, while—at the same time— we have direct connectivity through our smartphones and tablets, whether or not the company knows or likes it?) There's something to be said about the communal work space that the Ace Hotel offers: You never know who you are going to run into, who you are going to sit next to, or how being in a hypercreative and fully open work space might impact the way that we work.

What's more amazing is that it's actually very quiet in the Ace Hotel. So while you're sitting in an open space—practically shoulder-to-shoulder with a stranger—many people are blocking out the surroundings by wearing headphones. Headphones are the DO NOT DISTURB sign for the new generation of work. I'm reminded of the book *Quiet* by Susan Cain, which validates that there are two divergent forces at play here, and they are creating a fundamental rethink in how we go to work each day. One driving force is communal spaces: More and more businesses are breaking down cubicle walls and centralizing people in pods or workgroups. The other driving force is solitary spaces: spots for people to go to actually get the work done once the conversations and collaboration are over. This is the deep thinking and practical execution on the work that we have all agreed to.

In understanding this new world, we need to find a new space to get the work done.

Time to think. A place to think. Your own little space. Artists use studios. Great businesspeople have offices. As the world continues to untether because of laptops, tablets, mobile devices, and persistent connectivity, those studios and offices have become moving targets. Musicians can record from their laptops. Any businessperson with a mobile phone can make their art in the corner café. The truth is that we—as the next generation of workers—have never had a better time in our professions to be able to find the right space to come up with the right ideas. We no longer have to "go to the office" to get our work done.

Someone recently asked me how much time I actually spend at the office. The question gave me pause. Even though I have two Twist Image offices (in different cities) that I spend quite a bit of time in, for some reason I consider my MacBook Air, iPad, and iPhone my "real" office. I jokingly told one of my business partners that we should expense my iPhone under the "rent" category of our P&L. Over the years, the construct of a physical office means less and less to the business professional: Our ability to generate ideas, create, and think about the clients we work with and the industries we serve is increasingly less about where we physically are and much more about the people we are collaborating with and our access to the information or tools we need to create. More and more businesses today are beginning to think in a philosophically different way about what the "office" is.

UNLIMITED CAPACITY.

What do you need to turn your business ideas and thoughts into a reality? Do you need a desk, a phone, a filing cabinet, a lamp, some manila folders? It's time to reframe your thinking. Think about being a painter. Painting is hard. First, you need the money to buy all the materials (canvas, brushes, paints, easel...), then you need years of practice to understand the intricate techniques to nurture your spark and flow. All of the arts are like this, including filmmaking, music, photography, writing, and even the work that we do at our professional crafts. Many of us dabble in art (we create content online or comment on it), and while many won't count this as art (because many think of fine art when they think of art), it's astonishing to think about what technology has given us: It is a tremendous gift. What we now have in this gift is the ability to create and connect it to others with an unlimited capacity.

I love my MacBook Air (in fact, I'm writing with it right at this moment). As someone who used to switch computers a few times every year (always wanting something faster, lighter, thinner...), I find the MacBook Air to be—without question—the best laptop I have ever owned. But it's more than what it does...it's how it makes me feel. I look at the laptop and realize that if I were a painter, it would be like having every type of canvas, brush, paint, and color available to me (and easy to take anywhere and everywhere). *Unlimited choices to create.* As someone who likes to tinker with words, this MacBook Air offers me unlimited capacity to explore, come up with ideas for clients, and create words. So yes, technology blows me away because of the ability to ideate and create with tremendous power and speed. But it's about more than creation.

It would be amazing if all I could do was create with unlimited capacity, but I can actually do more. I can turn those words into a media channel. I can then distribute that media to the world (for free) instantly—as soon as the muse strikes. I can share it with the world...and the world can then engage in the discourse. Yes, this is one of those moments when we should all get a little sentimental about how profound technology is. It also forces me to realize that my work space is very much a digital environment.

This unlimited capacity actually breaks down divides. It changes how we define both the work that we do and the facade of an office. The lesson here is that everything has changed about our work space, and it is not clear what the future of the office will be (more purgatory). You see, it's not really a MacBook Air that I'm typing on: It's a tool of change. It's not just a way to connect, share, collaborate, and build business either. It's a tool that can (and should) eliminate mediocrity or the doldrums of everyday life. The lesson is about using this power to do something great—to not just sit in a Dilbert-like cubicle, but to actively think about what happens as the office becomes the digital office.

IBM has been challenging the notion of an office in very different and powerful ways. In the age of social media, they've been leveraging their own social media platform (which many have described as a Facebook for IBMers) called IBM Connections. With many offices all over the world and a ton of employees who not only telecommute but work as consultants, the true head office for IBM's powerhouse of thinkers has become IBM Connections. It enables each employee to have a Facebook-like profile, and includes the ability to create online communities, manage tasks, engage with the corporate wiki, and many other services (media galleries, the ability to create blog posts, and more).

The major functionality is the depth and search power behind the professional profiles of their team members. IBM has close to five hundred thousand employees and nearly one hundred thousand contractors, so these profiles offer information in a way that looks more like LinkedIn profiles on steroids than business cards. IBMers all over the world can access the private online social network to find colleagues within the organization who can help them do their jobs better. Let's say you're in need of someone in Sacramento with intranet skills. Not only can IBM Connections help make the introduction, but you can even learn more about people (including their families and whatever else these co-workers care to post). As the platform continues to evolve through functional additions and general usage, it is bringing IBM team members much closer together, while also making everyone—and the entire organization—a lot smarter.

It's no small feat and it comes with a hefty price tag, but that doesn't mean that these tools to connect are out of the grasp of businesses of every size. What's important to focus on is just how much the overall function of the office can morph when you add in a layer of continuous connectivity and encourage your team to share beyond standard conference calls and client meetings.

These new inclusions into our work space change the very fabric of our offices. We now have physical locations that look very different; a connectivity through mobile devices that allows us to work anywhere and everywhere; and platforms to keep us intimately closer to our team members and the projects that are being worked on and to provide us with an overall bird's-eye view of what's happening within the organization. The physical and digital realms begin to gel and morph.

THE FUTURE OF WORK AND SPACE.

In April 2008, *The Economist* ran an article titled "The New Oases," which looked at how our newfound mobility was in the process of redefining and changing our physical work spaces:

> In the 20th century architecture was about specialized structures—offices for working, cafeterias for eating, and so forth. This was necessary because workers needed to be near things such as landline phones, fax machines and filing cabinets, and because the economics of building materials favored repetitive and simple structures, such as grid patterns for cubicles. . . . Buildings will have much more varied shapes than before. For instance, people working on laptops find it comforting to have their backs to a wall, so hybrid spaces may become curvier, with more nooks, in order to maximize the surface area of their inner walls.

This is pretty amazing. In a world of fewer and fewer filing cabinets and bookcases, we're starting to see a surge in very prominent professionals who have no fixed address, even if they're working out of the same physical office space each day.

The asset management firm Russell Investments includes employees who have dubbed themselves "free-deskers." These individuals do not have assigned desks or offices. Each day, they sit down at whatever desk is made available to them. All of their contact information (phone, email, etc.) is 100 percent mobile. When you call a direct line, you reach that individual—no matter where they are seated in the office or where they are situated in the world.

What do you think this does to promote new thinking and moments of collision? At a macro level, desk floating also discourages office space as a status symbol. *We spent decades fighting for that corner office, and it now turns out that corner-office thinking is a thing of the past.* The newer offices have a different guiding principle: Work space is less about how much square footage each office has and how spacious it is as we now move toward a modernized space—one that is much more flexible in terms of use and more actively in tune with the digital nomad that is the new employee and the "anywhere" work space. Your office, the Ace Hotel, the study in your home—your office is everywhere.

LESSONS FROM WORKING THE NEW SPACE...

Lesson #1—The digital office.

This is a time of breaking the silos. More people are mobile, more people are untethered, and the most successful businesses are not just leveraging technology to make them better, they're integrating technology into every single aspect of their operations. This is a full-on digitization of the office space. Ultimately, this is not just about productivity and profits, but about creating the optimal work environment, because a better overall health creates more profit and productivity. People have been stuck worrying about the physicalness of their office—from the chairs they sit on to the desks they sit at, the structure of the physical environment, and the physical location of the building. It goes on to the types of phones that are used and the pens that are provided to write with. It seems like many people feel trapped by the physical aspects of their workplace when—deep down—it's actually the things that happen between the ears that matter most. Remove the workplace from the work. Enable and empower yourself to work from any place and every place because the new office is the laptop, smartphone, and tablet (and everything that powers them).

Lesson #2—Design for agility.

It's time to reboot how you think about your office and the office space. Your work space should be designed and structured for collaboration—and that's all. The office should be a space that fosters discussion (and even contrary positions) and decisions. Companies like Apple, Threadless, and even us—at Twist Image—design our spaces in a way that not only matches a corporate culture, but is built for a Ctrl Alt Delete world. It's a space that is designed for moments of collision: open, few closed doors, lots of sunshine, and whiteboards everywhere. The advertising agency 72andSunny—the hippest of hip new ones—has created a reputation by ensuring that national advertising campaigns can be in-market (start-to-finish) within a month. This type of work was unheard of in a pre-technology world, but it's not technology that is facilitating this reboot of the traditional advertising model . . . it is their physical space. The agency that works with clients like Nike, Activision, and Xbox 360 doesn't structure their teams by department, but rather by project. It's common to see the client services lead sitting next to the art director while the strategist and media planner sit in tandem. This structure reduces meetings and approvals by enabling an iterative collision of work to happen. The new office space also allows people to go off and get the work done. Even in open environments, remember that headphones are the new DO NOT DISTURB sign.

Lesson #3—Create more collisions.

Apple's new campus (which is due to be completed in 2016) will cover close to three million square feet and hold up to thirteen thousand Apple employees. The headquarters (based in Cupertino, California) will also house its own power plant and over six thousand trees. The design has been called a "spaceship," and reading the Steve Jobs biography by Walter Isaacson tells us there's a powerful reason for its circular shape: Steve Jobs loved moments of collision. The biography tells the tale of Pixar's headquarters where the bathrooms were something of a hike for the majority of employees. Pregnant women were known to complain and were said to speak in hushed tones about Jobs's lack of compassion, when—in reality—Jobs just wanted people to collide and spark conversations (yes, even on the way to the bathroom). This new "spaceship" campus is circular and all glass so that people can have more and more moments of collision.

Lesson #4—Better meetings.

Because technology, communication, and connectivity have changed everything, meetings—as we have known them—should change and will continue to evolve. More and more of us are engaged in video conference meetings and—as with any technology—there will be many false starts and mistakes made. Still: Don't let the technology make you less human. In fact, the best way to optimize meetings is to be as humane and civil as possible, whether you're in person or attending via webcam. Meetings have become one of the most loathed parts of people's work life. We now have a massive opportunity to return meetings to their glory and leverage these get-togethers as opportunities to push the business forward and to ensure that it does not stagnate. Leverage technology to make those advances, and get rid of the technology that is holding your meetings hostage.

Lesson #5—Social media connections.

For all the things that may still leave you skeptical of social media (massive time suck, people acting like jerks, narcissism on display...), there also lies a massive opportunity to use digital channels and platforms to connect the people you work with to one another and, yes, back down to the customer. While you may not have the ability to deploy a platform like IBM Connections, start thinking of ways to leverage social technology so that more people can understand not only who they are working with but what those people are working on. Social technology will not replace in-person meet-ups or mentoring initiatives, but it can and should be used as a way for everyone within your organization to get better acquainted with one another.

BEYOND THE OFFICE.

Understanding how to work in our rebooted world is to live and breathe in these new work environments. Think deeply about the following questions:

- What are we doing to make our office space more mobile?
- What are we doing to create more flexible spaces for people to collaborate?
- Do we have enough moments of collision and interaction between varying departments?

- Do we have enough breathing room for people to go off on their own and do the long, hard thinking and doing?
- How can we leverage social media to make our team members more personal and more connected?
- How can we create more shared spaces and resources?
- How does our office space foster a better work experience?
- What does our current office space say about our culture and who we are?
- How can we make our physical space more connected to the community that we serve?

These are the questions that you can now go off and think about as your business space continues to evolve.

CHAPTER 11

Your Life in Startup Mode

The shift from a job to the work that you were meant to do.

YOU ARE ABOUT TO LOSE YOUR JOB.

The majority of our world is filled with people who are concerned about their job . . . and if they are going to lose it. The lucky ones are concerned about how they're going to reach the next plateau or get their full bonus at the end of the year, but there's a huge swath of people who are mostly just trying to get by. These people are punching the clock and trying to make ends meet. They're less concerned about where they're going and much more concerned about not being let go from their jobs tomorrow. Beyond that, there are many people who are unemployed and would welcome the kind of misery that those clock-watchers are enduring. If you look at the global job market, things are not pretty.

That was the crux of Thomas L. Friedman's column on July 12, 2011, in the *New York Times* titled "The Start-Up of You." His premise? The job market is not going to get any better, because the jobs of yesterday are gone and the companies with big valuations (he names Facebook, Twitter, etc.) aren't looking for the types of workers that companies used to hire decades ago. Instead, these new companies are looking for smart engineers, but beyond that, it's all about "people who not only have the critical thinking skills to do the value-adding jobs that technology can't, but also people who can invent, adapt, and reinvent their jobs every day, in a market that changes faster than ever." It's a tall order, and one the universities and schools are rushing to catch up to.

It turns out that this seismic shift in how business is evolving forces the biggest of corporations to act more like startups. Pushing that even further, we're seeing true success come from those very smart individuals who are governing their own lives and careers as if these were a startup of one. To put that into perspective, we started our marketing agency in 2000 and—if you fast-forward to today—we've got several employees with job titles that didn't even exist when we first started our business. On top of that, these new job titles—driven by new and different kinds of work in a world of Ctrl Alt Delete—continue to be created.

There is a secret to business today that few of the major corporations will readily admit: You can do a whole lot with very little (as we have learned in the previous chapters of *Ctrl Alt Delete*). Many viable companies are made up of less than a handful of employees (remember the story of Instapaper's Marco Arment at the beginning of this book?). In Friedman's editorial, he makes it very clear: "You could easily fit all their employees together into the 20,000 seats in Madison Square Garden, and still have room for grandma. They just don't employ a lot of people, relative to their valuations, and while they're all hiring today, they are largely looking for talented engineers."

The time has come for each of us to get lean and start treating our squiggly career paths much more like startups. It's hard for people who have had traditional jobs to think like entrepreneurs, but now it's more critical than ever. As we discussed in a previous chapter, an entrepreneur is someone who is trying to create a future that doesn't yet exist, while a businessperson is someone who is trying to mitigate risk and minimize mistakes.

If you take that analogy and apply it to how you're guiding your professional development, where do you net out? The most valuable players on any corporate team are not the ones who are mitigating risks; the new breed is all about those who are adaptive, nimble, flexible, and creative (in everything that they do). It's not going to be part of the standard job description either; it will be the baseline for those who thrive versus those who only survive...maybe.

BEING A STARTUP OF ONE IS NO JOKE.

Louis C.K. is much more than a very popular comedian. He is a shrewd businessperson. He is actively hands-on in anything and everything that bears his name and he spends a tremendous amount of time ensuring that whatever he does (from TV shows to tours to comedy specials) represents his brand in the best possible light. He is known to get way down into the weeds of the work. For his television show he handles everything from editing down to the music selection.

On December 10, 2011, C.K. released his fourth full-length comedy special, *Live at the Beacon Theater*, but unlike his previous specials, he decided to run this project like an ultra-lean startup and distributed it digitally through his own website. *Leveraging the power of his direct relationship with his fans*, C.K. circumvented physical and broadcast media, publishers, producers, and distribution companies. He took a startup approach (including the participation in a Reddit AMA—Ask Me Anything—question-and-answer session online). Many of his peers and business associates warned him against releasing his content this way (C.K. pushed things further by making the special DRM-free so people could rip it to a DVD or the like) for fear that not only would he lose money, but his performance would be pirated and spread through the torrent sites. But C.K. made a personal plea on his website: "Please help me keep this being a good idea. I can't stop you from torrenting; all I can do is politely ask you to pay your five little dollars, enjoy the video, and let other people find it in the same way."

The results were astounding. As of late December 2011, the sales from the special earned him over $1 million (and growing). He leveraged the distribution of this digital-only special to announce a new album that he recorded at Carnegie Hall. Along with that came a mass amount of media coverage (both in the mainstream and online) lauding his startup spirit and how he leveraged technology to empower the direct relationships that he has nurtured over his years of growth. The success of this project prompted other comedians to follow suit. On May 11, 2012, C.K. launched two additional audio specials (also priced at $5 apiece) along with an audio-only version of the *Live at the Beacon Theater* event. While the majority of us may not be rising comedy stars, the power in C.K.'s decisions was in *not* following the standard operating procedures that all comedians follow (work the road, get a manager, get a television show, get a special, and continue on). Instead, he approached his career (and life) with that startup spirit: a rugged determination and belief in himself and his work and the ability to consciously pursue it with a bootstrapped mindset.

NOW IT'S YOUR TURN...

The January 2012 cover story of *Fast Company* magazine was all about Generation Flux. You've heard of Gen X, Gen Y, and more, but what is Generation Flux?

Our business world has been through some tumultuous times: recessions, financial meltdowns, the massive disruption of technology, natural disasters, nations defaulting on their debt, the Arab Spring, the Occupy Movement, and much more. From every catastrophe and massive shift emerge new breakthroughs and advancements. During these past few years, we've also seen some of the most interesting companies flourish and grow (Apple, Facebook, Lululemon, Amazon, Twitter, and more); we've seen medical advancements at an unprecedented pace and the introduction of new technologies that will forever change our future. In short, this is a time of flux and uncertainty... but a time of great innovation as well. This makes it hard to chart a course—let alone pull together a five-year plan. Have you taken a look at your investment portfolio recently? Do you honestly think that there is a reliable long view out there? It is within this sense of pandemonium that *Fast Company* has dubbed us—all of us—Generation Flux.

"To thrive in this climate requires a whole new approach," states the *Fast Company* article "This Is Generation Flux: Meet the Pioneers of the New (and Chaotic) Frontier of Business" by Robert Safian. "Some people will thrive. They are the members of Generation Flux.... What defines GenFlux is a mindset that embraces instability, that tolerates—and even enjoys—recalibrating careers, business models, and assumptions. Not everyone will join Generation Flux, but to be successful, businesses and individuals will have to work at it. This is no simple task. The vast bulk of our institutions—educational, corporate, political—are not built for flux. Few traditional career tactics train us for an era where the most important skill is the ability to acquire new skills."

These same notions of flux are core to governing your career like a startup business. Reid Hoffman, the co-founder of LinkedIn, must be some kind of oracle at this particular time in the history of business. With close to 140 million members in over twenty countries, LinkedIn held an IPO in May 2011 that made Hoffman a billionaire. Currently, he serves as executive chairman of LinkedIn and is a partner at Greylock Partners—a very successful venture capital firm. Hoffman's passion is in understanding how these connected networks that we're all creating every day as we friend, like, link, and follow one another create new business opportunities. He also believes that in these highly networked times, we have to start thinking differently about business and the work that we're doing. He and Ben Casnocha (an award-winning entrepreneur and author) published the book *The Start-Up of You: Adapt to the Future, Invest in Yourself, and Transform Your Career.*

"I was fascinated when I met people who were entrepreneurial but didn't want to necessarily start their own companies," said Casnocha. "That was my arrival at *The Start-Up of You* thesis. Reid had been thinking about the idea of everyone as a business of themselves. In many ways, the LinkedIn vision is a manifestation of the intellectual idea in the book. We had both been thinking about these ideas independently. . . . There is a convergence of two key trends happening now. First is a trend toward entrepreneurship. People are looking to people like Steve Jobs and other business icons as the great heroes of the world. Secondly, globalization, technology disruption, unemployment, job crisis, and this idea that the labor market is changing are making people feel less secure. This lack of security is causing people to ask the question: 'What do we do about it?' So people are looking toward the hot trend of entrepreneurship as the answer. While I think that people should start more companies, the reality is that not everyone is cut out for it. What can we do? We can learn from these dynamic entrepreneurs and figure out how to apply those lessons of success to our lives and careers."

What we're seeing is a world where the next generation is not looking for (or even concerned with) job security and a pension, but rather governing their careers and guiding their future by the lessons learned from some of Silicon Valley's most successful entrepreneurs and innovators. As more and more people leverage the thinking along the lines of what we're discussing in this chapter, they're now able to build their own powerful networks, turn to proactive risk taking (and don't see it as a risk, but rather an opportunity), and get very adaptive to the economic realities of a world where big business is no longer the preferred and revered career path. It makes you wonder if being a small startup (in your professional attitude and in how you run your day-to-day business) is the future of big business.

EMBODYING THE STARTUP MINDSET:

1. **Look to the edges.** Many people wrongly think that this startup mindset comes from the top down. It doesn't. More often than not, when you meet successful startup founders, their ideas and philosophies come from the edges. They are cultivated by moments of frustration or people who think, *Why don't we do things this way?* Be an individual who is looking at the edges of your business and your career, and what that business may look like in two to five years' time...and where you see yourself fitting in and adjusting your skill sets to be effective.

2. **Invest in yourself.** The majority of people who get in on a startup are taking significantly less salary in exchange for options in the company. This concept of vesting is critical. Having a startup mentality for your own career is the same. Invest in it and know that the likelihood of cashing out in a major way will happen in the future. It's not a lottery. The compensation for being a great startup does not come from the salary, it comes from the equity...and the sweat equity that you're putting into it.

3. **Align with the right people.** Successful startups usually have high turnover because people quickly realize that the lifestyle is not for them. Know that as you govern your own startup, the key to your success will come from not only who you are working with, but the people who advise and mentor you. Do everything you can to connect and learn from great mentors and advisers. Some of the best startups are the ones with a very strong board of directors. Create your own personal board of advisers.

4. **The lifestyle.** The lifestyle of a startup is a 24/7 lifestyle. Startup founders and team members are renowned for working tirelessly. Intense work. Sleeping on camping mattresses, eating delivery pizza, and slogging through marathon sessions to deliver and iterate on their product. When you're running a startup, you're not watching the clock—you're too focused on delivering a great product.

5. **Imposed deadlines.** In order to move things along, startups put a ton of pressure on themselves by creating imposed deadlines. The ability to iterate, create, and deliver under these self-imposed deadlines enables them to move faster. Yes, you want the work to be as smart as possible as well, because a smart startup makes the assumption that someone else, somewhere, is trying to solve the exact same problem. Impose deadlines on your own success and push yourself to beat those goals.

6. **Embrace mistakes.** Sadly, most businesses start with an idea and stick with it until the bitter end. For a tiny few, the end means making the *Fortune* 500 list, but for most it means either bankruptcy or some very disappointed investors. We live in a new era of entrepreneurship, and business ideas can be tested and marketed for success like never before. Eric Ries has been preaching the value of what he has called *The Lean Startup* in his very popular blog and bestselling business book

of the same name (published two years ago), and it has become all the rage. Much like Malcolm Gladwell's *The Tipping Point* became a catchphrase that every business executive used in 2002, over the past two years every person looking to start a business has been talking about it being a "lean startup." The most embraced concept in Ries's book was the notion of the "pivot": that the most successful startups (the ones that eventually turned a two-person operation into a multimillion- or multibillion-dollar business) were the ones that were able to identify quickly that what they were doing did not have much commercial viability and were able to "pivot" the business model—through iteration—into something people actually wanted to use. Ries masterfully taught startups to learn from their many mistakes by encouraging them to embrace the many mistakes—by acting on them.

7. **High risk.** For the most part, startups are doing something new and unproven. They're answering a question that nobody has thought to answer. The future is uncertain and this is very stressful—especially for people with a low tolerance for risk (which is the majority of the population). The global economy has not given us any key leading indicators that the job market can provide any semblance of security; nor has it been able to ensure those that have a low tolerance for risk that it can help them. A startup is, without question, a high-risk venture, but what choice do you have when looking at it in terms of your career? In this time of economic uncertainty, pretty much every career path is risky. The risk is also present because startups often change priorities on the fly, and ideas that were once given high priority can be abandoned when the plan changes. Think of your career in the same light: Just because you had a perception of what you should be doing after you graduated from college doesn't mean that your original

career path must be adhered to for the entire span of your career and personal development. Know that the world continues to fundamentally change, and we're still in the midst of this purgatory.

8. **Head down.** The startup mentality is not about the next promotion, job interview, raise, or vacation. The startup mentality is about being "head down." It's an understanding that there is a predefined goal that needs to be met. This is accomplished by setting out many smaller steps that will get you there. Have a keen understanding that every small detail is to be dwelled upon and that each small, successive step to the goal will need to be tweaked and iterated along the way. Head down. Stay the course.

YOU DON'T HAVE TO RUN A STARTUP TO ACT LIKE A STARTUP.

I believe that each of us has a startup inside. Each of us has looked at our businesses or an industry and had an idea or came up with an opportunity that could add value to consumers' lives. Does this mean that everybody should do a startup? To make a run at it, you need to have certain skills and a mentality (as defined above) of rugged individualism mixed with a panache for teams. Still, the bigger opportunity is to consider your life as a startup. To treat it as a nimble and exciting project that is going to go through many phases. If you look at numerous reports and surveys, they're now saying that university graduates of today will likely have between four and six career changes over the span of their lives. These are not job changes...they're career changes. There is no finish line to this process, and it will force you—day in and day out—to figure out how to get more lean, agile, and strategic in everything that you do.

Brutal. Down to the bone.

Imagine making a list of all of the things that you needed to accomplish, today, this week, this month, this quarter, and this year. The list could be as long as you like. Now go through that list and be ruthless. What if you could only do one thing today? What would it be? Individuals who run startups do this—on a day-to-day (sometimes moment-by-moment) basis. They're pre-revenue, they're hungry to prove themselves, and they have everything to lose. The truth is that these types of individuals rarely make it in a corporate setting, but the other truth is that many startups fail as well. There is a massive opportunity moving forward to look at your business as a unique startup and—at the same time—do the same thing with your own life and career. Those who govern themselves as startups will be the ones who not only survive but thrive through these ever-changing times.

A STARTUP MEANS YOU HAVE TO START SOMETHING.

The reason is simple: There's no longer any excuse to sit back and complain. Prior to social media, it was easy to read a newspaper column, disagree with the journalist, but then see yourself as an unheard voice in the media wilderness. But now—*for free*—the platforms exist for you to validate your thinking, not only by putting it out there but also by getting feedback from the community. In short, if you don't like something (anything), you can now start your own blog. So what are you waiting for? Start something...

I still believe that a blog is a canvas that allows you to think, share, and connect with an audience. You don't have to approach it with the mentality of turning it into the next *TechCrunch* either. The topic can be as obscure as your brain can fathom, and odds are that a blog covering that exact topic already exists. Pushing that further, it's hard to even define what, exactly, a blog is in this day and age. After all, you can blog on your Facebook page, you can micro blog with Twitter, or you can video blog on YouTube. You can even blog using tumblr—which is a hybrid online social network and blogging platform—or you can blog for an existing online publisher like the *Huffington Post*. But for the purpose of this book, I'll define a blog as an online journal of your work. The spirit of the blog is to create a living and breathing résumé and portfolio of how you think and work.

Here's how to start a blog in twelve easy(ish) steps:

1. **Choose the right platform.** The default choice for a great blogging platform is WordPress. My recommendation is to go with it (full disclosure: My blog is powered by MovableType and it's way too late in the game to make the switch to WordPress, but I would if it could happen seamlessly). Do the hard work of figuring out if a hosted solution is best for you. My general recommendation is to use the free version until you start seeing uptake by the community. No point in spending the money if you're not generating readership and/or going to stick with it.

2. **Design matters.** While we do live in a world of RSS feeds and links tossed around via Facebook, Pinterest, LinkedIn, and Twitter, the best blogs are designed well. They look good and read well. WordPress makes this (somewhat) easier because you can buy and customize themes. If you're serious about blogging, get very serious about having it look great. It's hard for people to get excited about a plain blog. Also, make sure that it's easily read on mobile devices and tablets. WordPress has plug-ins to help you get it right. Design matters. Always.

3. **Great names.** It can be funny, quirky, or a play on an existing meme, but figure out a relevant, cool, and timely name for your

blog. I believe that people like saying *Six Pixels of Separation* much more than *Mitch's Blog*. Finding a name is never easy, but when it's done well, it makes the blog much more sharable. People like sharing things that not only sound cool, but make them look smart. The blog's name matters. Try to avoid multiple-word titles where one word's last letter is the same as the next word's first (like: mikesstand). You're trying to make it easy, not confusing, for people to find you.

4. **Secure your domains.** In a world where finding a domain name can become an expensive and frustrating endeavor, refer to the last bullet point as your guiding light: The more unique, strange, and funky the title, the more likelihood you'll have of being able to secure the URL. A trick would be to use one of the more reputable domain name websites to see if your choice is available prior to choosing it (and if it is, please make sure to grab it on the spot—you don't want to come back a week later and find that someone else already bought it).

5. **Write a full bio.** I've seen countless WordPress bio pages that are simply left blank. Be sure to write a full bio and make it as robust as possible. People want to know whom they're reading. Make it crisp and clever. A great bio (with direct contact information) is critical.

6. **Read first.** Most people will tell you to start writing. I would argue that if you want to start a blog, first start by reading. Read everything. Blogs, books, newspapers, magazines, tweets... Get a feel for the industry that you're going to blog about and form your own perspective. Along with that perspective, it's equally fine for you to start commenting in other online spaces before starting your own blog. Commenting on more heavily trafficked sites will give you insights into how people feel about your way of thinking (especially if your comments get other people excited about commenting and adding to the discourse).

7. **Write. Write. Write.** If you want a successful blog, you have to write. You have to write a lot, and you have to post frequently. You have to do this not to simply cram content into a blog, but because only through the frequency and habit of writing will you get good at it. Only through the frequency and habit of writing will you begin to find a voice. Only through the frequency and habit of writing will you begin to build an audience. Here's a truth: You won't find your voice over time. I don't believe that writers arrive at this strange destination called "their voice." I think a strong voice evolves over time. But none of that happens without writing. You're not writing for writing's sake. *You're writing to exercise your critical thinking skills.* When you do that often enough, great writing will start to flow.

8. **Watch what you write.** Spelling and grammar count. I recently came across a new blog that was started by a lawyer (it said so in the bio). It was littered with spelling and grammar mistakes. I type fast and I make mistakes (and there is a great group of people who send me notes and leave comments so that I can correct my mistakes), but overall, the flow of the writing has to at least be readable. I'm not talking about random misspellings or grammatical burps (it happens). I'm talking about text that is unreadable (and in truth, somewhat laughable). Poor spelling and bad grammar undermine your content and your critical thinking. Take the time to either proof your own work or find someone who will take pity on you and do it. Spelling and grammar mistakes will directly affect your credibility. Trust me on this.

9. **Don't be shameless about self-promotion.** Whenever it's time to promote my blog, I get a pit in my stomach. I love blogging, I love sharing, but I hate beating my own chest. Choose how you're going to self-promote, but before you do

anything ask yourself: *If this message showed up in any one of my streams, how would I feel about it?* As a way to not feel too self-promotional, I use my other social media spaces for self-promotion by asking a question on Twitter and Facebook in the hope of provoking some kind of reaction on the blog in response to my post. This feels like I'm adding value to someone's stream without it being a *Look at me! Look at me!* moment.

10. **Don't be scared of analytics.** Most blog platforms offer some kind of analytics. You should also be running Google Analytics. If the thought of Web analytics scares you, please go and check out the work of Avinash Kaushik (his blog, *Occam's Razor*, is a treasure trove of great insights, as are his two books *Web Analytics: An Hour a Day* and *Web Analytics 2.0*). You should be measuring everything from readership and referral traffic to keywords. I particularly like keyword analysis, because this can give you some immediate insights into the type of words people use to find your content. Write more with those keywords in mind.

11. **Take it slow.** It is quick, free, and easy to build a blog, but building an audience and finding that elusive voice is a long, hard, and desperately lonely journey. Make sure you are ready for it. There will be times when you will question if anybody is reading your blog and if anybody cares. It's not easy, but keep at it. If you believe that you have something useful to share, odds are that there are others—just like you—out there as well. I have been blogging for over a decade and have a lot of readers, and still, to this day, I wonder if anybody really cares (like, what would happen if I stopped blogging tomorrow?). It's fine and normal to have those feelings, but keep at it. Why? Because if you care enough to blog, it means that you have something to say. If you have something to say and

you're blogging it, it means that you want to share and connect. Ultimately, the world needs more people like that.

12. **Get started.** Be patient and really start out slowly to make the changes feel like they're not changes at all. Starting slowly will also help you define if this is a talent of yours or something that needs to be readjusted. I bet you can find something to start with today: How about committing to watching one hour less of TV every week and spending that hour reading about the industry you serve? My guess is that within one to two months, you'll be in love with the work that you do or you'll be looking for a place that better defines your talent and passion.

LESSONS FROM THE STARTUP OF ONE...

Lesson #1—The risk is real.

There is no time like the present to embrace the startup mentality. No jobs are safe because very few industries are safe. Everything—as we have known it to date—is going through a massive shift in digitization and mobility. This changes everything. The reality is that some of the biggest organizations in the marketplace today are actually hiring fewer and fewer people because they simply need less people to generate the same kinds of revenue.

There is no doubt that the fastest-growing sector in the North American economy is being driven by anything and everything that touches Silicon Valley—the hotbed for startups. The challenge is that the biggest and brightest in this industry (Google, Facebook, Twitter, Kickstarter, LinkedIn...) simply do not employ a lot of people in relation to their valuations. Yes, the majority of these companies have many job openings, but they are for technical and engineering posts. The fact remains that the biggest companies are doing more with a lot less. Thinking like a startup is a skill set that will get you through the next half decade.

Lesson #2—Treat your life like a startup.

Remind yourself of how Louis C.K. examined his business and made a serious decision to govern his own destiny. This doesn't mean that you should quit your job tomorrow and go it alone. It means that there's no reason not to start thinking about and treating your life like a startup, even if you're getting up and going to the office every day. The startup mentality is one where you are actively taking a hands-on approach to your own professional outcome.

Lesson #3—Sorry, no gold watch.

There are countless lessons to be learned from looking at the type of people and companies that were featured in *Fast Company* magazine's Generation Flux cover story. And that was only the tip of the iceberg. In your current role, do you have faith that after twenty years of solid service you will retire with benefits to that white-picket-fenced house out in the country? Are you really counting on the send-off dinner where you will be given a plaque commemorating your service . . . or that gold watch?

I think (hope) that you now realize there's no gold watch in your future.

Lesson #4—Embrace the mindset.

You don't have to run a startup to run your career like a startup, but you do have to embrace and embody the mindset. Startups are not from the top down; rather, the attitude comes from the edges. And the best are those where people are vested in terms of their time, money, and effort. This isn't a mad, short run at some additional cash. It's a dream of something much bigger. Figure out who you need to align yourself with: mentors, advisers, friends, and beyond. It's a time to set up and live by self-imposed deadlines to make things happen, while always being open to the reality that the mistakes you make along the way are going to be the defining moments. You should take comfort in understanding that the future is always about being head down into your work because everything in business has suddenly become high-risk. Don't fear it. Embrace it.

Lesson #5—Be brutally honest with yourself.

It's going to be hard. It's going to be tough. It's going to be challenging, but it will be the most rewarding thing you will do in your professional career. Start treating your career like the startup that it deserves to be. Within all of this, you will no longer be worried about things like when the next lunch break is or why the person sitting next to you doesn't get reprimanded for coming to work late and leaving early. You will be in a state of flow and you will be working toward the ultimate goal: personal success and fulfillment.

A STARTUP MINDSET IS A LEADERSHIP MINDSET.

There's an often discussed paradox of the startup mindset that attempts to quantify which trait is more important for business: being the first or being the best? The challenge (which seems rather obvious to me) is that everyone would choose to be the best (if given the choice). But it's hard to find any real data to suggest that the majority of those who are considered "the best" are the ones who weren't the first (the leaders), but rather those who sat back and waited for the market to mature before swooping in and taking control of it. It's also easy to be an armchair quarterback.

Famed blogger and business author Chris Brogan (who co-authored *Trust Agents* and *The Impact Equation* with Julien Smith and released a book called *Social Media 101*) launched a business book called *Google+ for Business: How Google's Social Network Changes Everything* long before Google+ was even allowing business to be all that active in their online social network. When Brogan first announced the book, he took some heat because fellow business pundits felt that it was way too early for anyone to publish a book on the topic with any semblance of credibility. In one blog post, Craig Peters (a fellow marketing professional) said, "My advice: Calm down. Let the slightly significant something be absorbed by both the marketplace and the marketplace of ideas. Then step back and take a look and see if it's worth all that and a bag of chips. Takeaway for marketers: Sometimes being the best is better than being the first."

When it comes to the world of startups, someone needs to be at the edge.

Regardless of whether or not Google+ becomes the next big thing, I don't think that Brogan is betting on Google+ so much as he is betting on being a leader in this new media space. Brogan's posture and business positioning are all about leadership in these connected channels. They're not about sitting idly by and then suddenly jumping on something once it becomes popular. He's the early settler, a pioneer . . . the one who is clearing the path for the rest of us. It's easy to call these people crazy or misinformed (imagine what everyone must have thought of Christopher Columbus in the 1400s). No, Chris is no Christopher Columbus, but he does walk the talk. He gets in early, explores, spends the time, pushes to see what it all means to businesses, and shares what he's thinking in such a candid way that those who aren't aligned are quick to pounce. Of course he won't always be right (don't get me started on how wrong I was about Second Life, Groupon, and others), but isn't that the point?

It's too bad that we're so quick to dismiss and not applaud those who take a startup position. Do you remember what people said about Twitter, YouTube, Facebook, and even Google in the early days? Do you remember what people said about MySpace, Cuil, and Friendster in the early days? The discourse was (pretty much) the same: No one could envision the business or business model. Do you think we would have had half the innovations that have changed our lives had those with the startup mindset sat back and not tried to be first in their market? Should we all wait for market research or a white paper before moving forward? The point is that the majority of people will sit back and wait for something to prove itself before moving forward, but there are also a handful of people who must take the risks and lead for us. My takeaway? That it's okay if you're not willing to take the risks. A lot of those risk-takers will be wrong. But that being said, your industry and your business probably need more innovation and risk-takers. *I think that should be you.*

IF FEAR IS HOLDING YOU BACK...

Just watch this: http://mashable.com/2012/06/04/buddy-media -ceo-makes-video/

CHAPTER 12

Embracing the Next

From purgatory to heaven...
what can we expect next?

WHAT NOW? WHAT'S NEXT?

When I first announced the title of this book, *Ctrl Alt Delete*, I had many people comment back, "What does that mean? After all, I use a Mac! And I don't even use a computer anymore; I'm on an iPad or an iPhone!"

The half joke was not lost on me. For years, the keys Ctrl Alt Delete denoted the reboot of a Windows-based personal computer. Besides, for a catchy book title, Apple's Command Option Esc just didn't have the same ring to it, and neither did "power button."

But as this book became a reality, I began to realize that the formal power button has now become our collective reboot (no matter what kind of device you're tinkering with). In short, when something goes wrong: reboot. So what now? What's coming next? The next is where business gets interesting. The next is where businesses get beyond the bright, shiny object that technology, social media, and mobility have become and move us into a place where we can actually think, invent, and plot the future of our business. Here are six forward-thinking trends to watch as we move from purgatory to the Promised Land...

THE NEXT #1—HACKER CULTURE EVERYWHERE.

What the world needs now is more hackers. Do you think that traditional mass media companies are really going to invent the future of media? It doesn't look good for them. The *Huffington Post* is often cited as one of the great disrupters of traditional journalism and media, but in truth, it's more ideologically aligned with the culture of hacking than it is with the evolution of journalism.

No, we're not talking about the type of hacking that caused cyber attacks on Sony's PlayStation Network, or the mythical characters that Anthony Weiner blamed when he tweeted out pictures of his own wiener. If you look at the true definition of a hacker, what you'll uncover is that there is a complimentary description of the term. The more complimentary description from Wikipedia states: "Someone messing about with something in a positive sense, that is, using playful cleverness to achieve a goal." Hacking away at something in small chunks or reprogramming bits and pieces of the media is what will define the future of media. It's also what will define the future of whatever industry you serve. Soon enough, every business will be in the business of hacking and employing hackers to reimagine the next generation of business models.

On May 23, 2011, a blog post titled "Reporting Live from the Scene of Breaking News...on an iPhone," from the Nieman Journalism Lab blog, went mostly unnoticed. It's too bad. It turns out that a company called Tieline Technology released an iPhone app called Report-It Live, which enables reporters, announcers, or anyone else for that matter to record, broadcast, and manage field reporting. While that might not sound like a big deal, you can head over to the Nieman Journalism Lab blog post to hear a sample of the sound quality from a standard phone connection being broadcast over the radio—and then the quality that their app can produce. It will not only stop you dead in your tracks in terms of audio quality, but you'll wonder why the traditional telecommunications companies never thought of an app this clever.

Hackers are creating our future. The future is about hackers in every industry.

The mistake most companies make is in thinking that hackers are great for brainstorming and creating crude versions of things, but anything of quality needs a more professional level of finesse and tender loving care to be viable in the modern world. Tell that to Facebook, Craigslist, Wikipedia, eBay, Instagram, and many others. All of these initiatives started off with a handful (or less) of people with an idea, a crude mockup, and a hacker's mindset of tinkering with an industry's problems until they arrived at some solution. In some instances, that "solution" still looks and feels crude to the traditional companies who have dominated that industry for decades (too bad for them).

It seems like Judy Shapiro (chief brand strategist at Cloud-Linux and blogger at *Trenchwars*) was busy asking herself some very similar questions at the TechCrunch Disrupt conference in New York last year. In her *Advertising Age* op-ed piece "When Hacker Culture Collides with Business Reality," she sees some major opportunities for marketing companies that my industry is not pursuing, and—because marketers are not doing anything about it—they are all but allowing (and enabling) small startups to take them on: "While the tech boys are breaking their toys—it is often the professional marketers (aka adults) who are left cleaning up the operational mess brought on by a lack of metrics and operational scalability. This culture collision starts to explain why marketers are facing tech fatigue and why Facebook's IPO languished. Just maybe, investors were unconvinced that Facebook could deliver the marketing goods since marketers themselves are getting weary of cleaning up the messes."

In sum, it's not about adults versus startups. The truth hurts, but here it is: The majority of marketing professionals are scared of technology. My guess is that the majority of leaders in your industry are scared of technology too. They don't understand it. They don't play with it. They would much rather leave the technical work to programmers and those with IT degrees than spend the time to deep-dive into what a new platform or channel can do to disrupt and change your industry. Hacking is quickly moving beyond the dorm rooms and garages of keeners trying to change the world. If you—the business leader—don't start pulling up your socks and embracing technology, innovation, hacker culture, and the startup culture, we're going to set our industries on a course for extinction.

Making the hacker culture work for you.

It would be wonderful to say, "No problem, let's just embrace this whole 'technology' thing and move on!" As we all know, change is hard (especially as your business begins to flourish). Ultimately, as technology connects more people and as more people become content creators and curators, our jobs moving forward will be in how we integrate a hacker culture into our business. This is equally important because two additional future trends are intrinsically linked with the hacking culture:

1. **3D printing.** Imagine being able to "print up" a three-dimensional product in much the same way you hit the print button for your word processing software. The hacker culture has given rise to many startups and centers of innovation within major corporations that are tinkering with the printer

of the future. This printer doesn't put images and words on paper, but actually creates physical objects. The current limitations of the technology (both hardware and software) make it as crude as the early days of dot matrix printing, but groups like MakerBot are running Hackathons to demonstrate the power and potential of 3D printing. Business is going to change dramatically when making three-dimensional solid objects from a digital file is as simple as hitting "command P" on your keyboard. A business's ability to produce rapid prototypes and to sell individualized products to consumers will create the next generation of upheaval. This is a profound change and can be witnessed in how the medical field is currently prototyping body parts and more using 3D printing. Imagine a world—in the not too distant future—when a failing kidney can simply be replaced by a healthy one that was just printed up on one of these printers. This type of innovation is already in development.

2. **Maker Movement.** In 2006, an event called Maker Faire was born. What can only be described as a contemporary subculture, this annual event showcases "makers"—people who create robotics, electronics, woodworking, 3D printing, and more. These hobbyists embody the next generation of the same philosophical ideologies that brought together people interested in computers and computing back in the 1970s at computer clubs and meetups (the places that people like Bill Gates and Steve Wozniak used to hang out). What's now being worked on in these garages and shared at events like Maker Faire is a combination of invention and prototyping. We're evolving from computer hardware and software into more tangible things (concept cars, robots, and more). The Maker Movement is closely tied to the rise of hackers, and people like Tim O'Reilly (founder of O'Reilly Media and advocate of the

free software and open-source movements) have described these events as the most exciting ways to see what the future holds for humanity. O'Reilly's company started publishing the magazine *Make* not only to highlight this new movement but to encourage everyone (including you) to start thinking about becoming a Maker. The Maker Faire now draws crowds of close to seventy thousand people annually and has spurred similar smaller events in many major cities around the world. For more on this, check out Chris Anderson's book *Makers: The New Industrial Revolution*.

THE NEXT #2—HORIZONTAL MARKETING.

Marketing must stop being vertical within a business and become horizontal across all business lines. Period. End of sentence.

Yet curiously, businesses fundamentally see the concept of social business as a fad. As if, suddenly, the employees within their organization will no longer be connected to one another and will no longer be engaged on a smartphone or tablet (meaning they will stop being hyperconnected in a completely untethered world). It's somewhat laughable that we still have corporations that block their employees from channels like YouTube and Facebook, when all employees have to do is put their hand into their pocket to be connected to those channels and platforms. From the public-facing side, consumers are beyond having expectations that a business should be social.

In fact, if a business isn't social, it's a nonstarter for many consumers. (Don't believe me? Just look at the discourse online regarding any brand. The majority of the conversation is around a lack of service and communication from said brand.) Do you do any business with companies that treat you like a number? We all still do (think about banks, cable companies, airlines, telecommunications firms, and a few others). Now, think about how many of those industries are engaged and connected in these channels and how it has fundamentally changed the way the public perceives them.

While this is painting with very broad strokes, it comes down to vertical integration versus horizontal integration. When a business claims to be moving in the direction of becoming a more *social business*, the brands that often fail are the ones that have a social media department within another department (usually marketing and/or communications); their work involves things like campaigns currently in-market or individual initiatives. This, in essence, is the ghettoization of the social business spirit and will ultimately lead to failure. When it's implemented horizontally (across all departments), you have a top-down and bottom-up seismic shift that becomes a value-based system by which the corporation is governed. In plain English: Everyone has skin in the game. *It's not a campaign, it's who you are—as a business.* It's a statement to the world that your business is made up of people and your consumers are people too. People do magnificent things in business when they can have real interactions between real human beings.

It's up to you to make the call and to make marketing a horizontal instead of a vertical.

Marketing directors wanting to implement social components into their business are unlikely to change the world, because it has to come from the top and run in symphony with everyone else. In short, it has to come from you or be led by you. Social business touches everything from human resources and operations to business development and product development. The major record labels within the music industry are making their struggles even worse because they don't have a social business framework. They were always in control (of the artists, of the music's distribution channel, of what the fans would hear), and they took that power on with the kind of pretentious attitude that is similar to how kings used to rule their empires.

When the C-suite makes the call, everything changes. Don't believe me? Just ask Tony Hsieh over at Zappos, Richard Branson at Virgin, or Marc Benioff at Salesforce.com. These business leaders (and there are many more) didn't sell social business through their organizations as a marketing and communications initiative. They sold it through as *customer service*. We're not talking about customer service in terms of the call center, we're talking about the core of customer service: Why are we in business?

We are in business to serve the customer.

Nothing more. Nothing less. The more we attempt to resist social business models, the more painful these next few years (and decades) will be. We can expect more local, more mobile, and more socially enabled consumers. The reality of the future is simple: *Again, all businesses must be social.* If you don't turn marketing into a horizontal that runs pervasively throughout the organization, your competitors will. And when they do, they will not only eat your lunch but they will marry your beloved consumers.

Want an excellent primer on social business and customer service? Pick up a copy of the blockbuster bestseller *Delivering Happiness* by Tony Hsieh. You'll get a terrific understanding of how and why Zappos has become beloved by its millions of customers.

THE NEXT #3—RISE OF THE INDIE BRAND.

In March 2012, I had the pleasure of delivering the opening keynote address at the Art of Marketing event in Toronto. With more than fifteen hundred business professionals in attendance, I shared the stage with people like Martin Lindstrom (author of *Brandwashed* and *Buyology*), Randi Zuckerberg (former head of marketing at Facebook and sister of its founder, Mark Zuckerberg), Scooter Braun (music industry professional and the person who discovered and manages Justin Bieber), and many others. The day-long, fully sold-out event featured seven top-of-their-game speakers and marketing professionals, but one individual stole the show. Eric Ryan is the co-founder (with his business partner, Adam Lowry) and chief brand architect of Method. Method is on a mission to totally change the consumer packaged goods business.

Their cleaning supplies are green, nontoxic, and so aesthetically pleasing that people display them with pride instead of hiding them under their sinks. They brand the company as "people against dirty" and leverage their indie brand street cred to push the envelope with everything from how they recruit (they give potential employees homework assignments) to their marketing (very clever and inventive uses of media with lots of humor) and their innovative product lines (check out their laundry detergent—it requires only a couple of squirts per load).

How well has it worked out for Method? Take a quick read of their bestselling business book, *The Method Method: Seven Obsessions That Helped Our Scrappy Start-Up Turn an Industry Upside Down,* which Ryan and Lowry co-wrote along with Lucas Conley.

How does an independent brand like Method rise in a business world where eight-hundred-pound gorillas like Unilever, Procter & Gamble, and Johnson & Johnson roam the jungle?

The answer is both complex and simple. The simple part is that our world has changed. Technology (and, more important, the Internet) has not only connected us all, but also opened up many new channels to better understand the nuanced needs of the modern consumer. The complexity comes in breaking down what all of this means. We now live in a world where online platforms like Kickstarter are enabling everyone to create a brand with global attention. We're quickly moving into a DIY (do it yourself) culture (look back to The Next #1 to see what hackers and makers are up to), where businesses can literally do everything and anything because of the power of the Internet—from sourcing production facilities to securing funding to cheap and effective direct-to-consumer marketing. All of this is giving rise to more individuals who are opting for entrepreneurship over the grind of the traditional nine-to-five.

The rise of independent companies developing and growing into world-class brands became a topic that fascinated an Amsterdam-based communications professional, Anneloes van Gaalen. For over three years, van Gaalen had been researching the rise of independent brands on a global scale and published her findings in a book called *Indie Brands—30 Independent Brands That Inspire and Tell a Story*. "The term 'indie brand' means a lot of different things to different people," said van Gaalen. "To me, this is about brands that are started by entrepreneurs that are independently funded and they have an independent spirit. These are the brands that go left when everyone is turning right. These are brands that make use of storytelling as their primary form of marketing . . . not advertising. They also make smart use of the available marketing channels. The brands that are in this book are people who started a business out of pure passion and they tend to opt for the road less travelled. This usually makes for an interesting story, and in this case, we published thirty of these interesting stories."

Riffing on the rise and future of the indie band movement, van Gaalen tells the story of thirty brands that manage to tell a very different narrative. From companies like OAT Shoes (the world's first fully biodegradable sneaker, which has seeds embedded in the tongue of the shoes, so when they are worn out, they can be buried and plants will grow) to the Yellow Bird Project (an organization that collaborates with indie bands to raise money for various charities and has published two bestselling books—*The Indie Rock Coloring Book* and *The Indie Rock Poster Book*). "We built this company from the ground up, without having to get any upfront investment," said Casey Cohen, who along with Matthew Stotland founded Yellow Bird Project in 2006. "This means that we're able to run this company on our own terms. We don't have partners to answer to, so any decisions that we make are final. This gives us the freedom to explore new directions, or even turn down opportunities that we think are not a good fit. At the end of the day, we spent so much time developing our brand that we're in a very fortunate position now to have complete control over it. Our charities and bands trust us, so we know that to them it just wouldn't feel right to be putting their trust into the hands of other people."

All of this leads to a very different business world. It turns out that the future will be less about brands that just tell a good story than it is about those that are transparent, credible, and have something unique and different for their consumers. Indie brands are starting to be born and bred on these values and principles, so it's no surprise that the major corporations that dominate Wall Street are now trying to figure out how to act more like Method, OAT Shoes, and the Yellow Bird Project. The next will happen as indie brands become the new big.

THE NEXT #4—LESS-IS-MORE MARKETING.

The future will not be about the brands that publish more and more product content. What do you really think consumers want:

to have that much more engagement with your brand, or to have an easier, simpler, and faster experience?

While you may think that those two areas are not mutually exclusive, they are actually intrinsically connected. If you can make the purchase funnel for your consumers have as little friction as possible, they'll become loyal. With that loyalty comes more engagement (sometimes). It's not as obvious as you may think. Most brands are cramming more and more pieces of content (which is mostly thinly veiled marketing pap) into more and more channels, but they're spending less and less energy making their own websites and platforms easier and faster for consumers to navigate.

In the future, every second counts.

Avinash Kaushik, whom I've referred to earlier, likes to remind audiences that for every second a person has to wait for a page to load on a website or mobile device, the conversion potential drops 7 percent. Consumers are unforgiving. They want efficiency and speed . . . not a cool Facebook page. And that is going to increase as the future unfolds.

Last May, *MarketingVox* ran a news item titled "Users Want Ease of Decision More than Engagement." It turns out that online shoppers couldn't care less about engaging with their favorite brand (unless they have a complaint or need more information). In fact, they'll switch (and fast) to a competitive brand that helps them buy faster.

In a study of 7,000 consumers and marketing executives representing 125 consumer brands across 12 industries, CEB identified a significant disconnect between current marketing strategies, including customer engagement, and preferred consumer buying behavior. While most marketers are behaving as if the majority of consumers are open to having a relationship with their brand, CEB found only 20% of consumers report being open to such relationships. As a result, today's marketing tactics are making customers less loyal, resulting in lost revenue for companies. "Our research indicates that the impact of simplifying purchase decisions for consumers is four times stronger than the favored marketing strategy of engagement and is the number one driver of likelihood to buy," said Patrick Spenner, managing director at CEB. "Too much choice and information causes customers to over-think purchase decisions, making them more likely to change their minds about a product, be less confident in their choice and less likely to repurchase."

Take a look at your marketing teams and ask this simple question: Who among us is responsible for ensuring that our consumers can get in, find what they need, and convert as quickly and efficiently as possible? Marketing optimization tends to look at opportunities within the campaign realm (how do we make these display ads flashier so people click on them?), but we can't forget about how critical it is to ensure that our entire experience is seamless and easy (and yes, it's an iterative and ongoing process). It's a cluttered Web, and it's going to get that much more cluttered and confusing as the devices get smaller, more untethered, and more mobile. *The future is going to be about speed for brands and not just about the quantity of content that they are producing and publishing.* Marketing and advertising are more important than ever before.

To date, we have made a mess of things. Most brands have no cohesive brand narrative because they're busy updating their websites with more pages, tweeting randomly on Twitter, working a Facebook page, experimenting on Pinterest, loading up videos on YouTube, and more. They're just throwing content at popular channels without looking at the holistic space and opportunity to extend a brand narrative. Even if they've nailed that down tight, they still struggle with simplicity: making their websites (mobile, Web, and touch) move quickly and efficiently. Google's homepage looks the way it does for a reason (same with Twitter, YouTube, Facebook, and beyond). They know that the simpler and faster they make their products, the less likelihood there will be for consumers to go elsewhere. The business world of the future is a place where brands publish less but optimize more for speed and efficiency.

Legacy thinking will play a major role in this.

It's easy to post to Twitter or to update your Facebook status. Not much to think about. But just because something is easy doesn't mean you shouldn't think about it.

I'm often asked why I don't post more personal information in the digital channels about my life (marriage? children? and so forth . . .). The truth is that my work and my business are intensely personal. I spend the majority of my waking days working, growing Twist Image, trying to build my ever-changing vision of how I define success. I use the digital spaces to focus on that area of my life (and, believe me, I take it very personally). In the creation of content (whether it's a book, blog post, podcast, or simple tweet), I often think about not only who will read it, but—more important—how it will be perceived long after I am dead.

So before anything gets published, I ask two questions:

1. Will this content stand the test of time?
2. Will my children (and their children) be proud of their father (grandfather) when looking at this?

This is why I don't (or try not to) use bad language, attack individuals, beat brands up, and more. It's not the reputation I want ... it's not the legacy I want to leave. This is particularly true of my audio podcast.

Think about it this way: In forty years, any one of your future family members will be able to go back in time and chronologically see everything (Mark Zuckerberg is on to something with the Facebook timeline) in sequential order ... blog posts, podcasts, tweets, updates, and more. It won't just be a shoe box of pictures and memories ... we're talking about a rich trove of content in text, images, audio, and video. Everything. These future generations will literally be able to know you—how you were feeling at a moment in time—and measure that against major moments in our history (think: 9/11, the Arab Spring, Occupy Wall Street, and beyond).

If you're a social business, this long-range concept should really blow your mind when you start to think about it.

The future of your business is about making your legacy mean something.

How often do you think about how your cumulative online persona is a reflection of your true character? We're going to be the first generation to have this kind of documented, individual history that is online for the world to see. Forever.

Most of the great leaders in our history don't have this kind of raw documentation available for the masses to view and review. Brands must start thinking about this and start taking this very seriously. The next level of marketing and communications will be about respecting this powerful publishing medium (and not just spamming). With every piece of content published, brands will begin to understand and respect the value of their consumers' time. Couple that with the legacy factor and brands will start to wake up and realize that everything they're doing today will be read and consumed decades and centuries from now.

What if we'd had these kinds of tools in biblical times? Imagine the kind of discourse we would have had around emerging religions and conquerors. Or what if we'd had these kinds of tools as the Industrial Revolution took hold? Imagine the kind of discourse we would have around the power of communications and media.

Imagine that we—each of us—had this power right now. But of course, we do. It's in the palms of our hands...literally. The true power comes from understanding the legacy this leaves. The easy thing to do is to dismiss the legacy (and power) and simply turn it into an engine of mindless spam. Unfortunately, that's what brands are doing now. The hard thing to do is to create content that creates a legacy. That's where brands are headed (hopefully).

THE NEXT #5—CONTROLLING TECHNOLOGY.

There's no doubt that technology brings with it some scary things. The scariest of them all is that of uncertainty. Human beings are creatures of habit, and any introduction of anything new typically raises an eyebrow (at least) or pitchforks (more often). If you study history, many of the same arguments that are made today as to why the Internet is ruining our society and culture are similar to the ones that were brought forth when we first saw the introduction of public speaking, the printed word, television, and on and on.

The common complaint about smartphones and mobile devices is that they are shackles that handcuff employees to their work—twenty-four hours a day and seven days a week. While your boss may have an expectation that because you have an iPhone, you should be responding to emails at 6 a.m. on a Saturday (emergency or not), this is less about your boss's disposition and more about a common lack of education as to how to use technology to get the best results. Many people are shocked to hear that my iPhone never makes a peep. I get one silent vibrate for text messages (and I'm quick to block those that I do not know) and two vibrations for a phone call. My iPhone will not beep, vibrate, or blink when emails, tweets, or Facebook updates arrive. Why? Because it's my job to best manage my technology (and not the other way around).

There's a macro lesson here: If you think your kids are spending too much time on your iPad and not enough time outside getting some exercise, don't blame the iPad. Before the iPad, they were playing video games, and before video games they were watching TV, and before TV they were reading comic books. Throughout history, you will uncover generations of youth who would rather sit around on their butts and play than go outside and play.

The Waldorf School of the Peninsula is one of over one hundred fifty Waldorf schools in the United States that don't allow technology or gadgets for students up until the eighth grade. These are not the wired classrooms we keep hearing about. In fact, they're traditional classrooms—the ones you might see in a Norman Rockwell painting (yellow pencils, wooden desks, and all). The reason why this particular school has received so much attention is because it is located in the heart of Silicon Valley and hosts children whose parents work at companies like Google, Yahoo!, and Apple. It seems so counterintuitive that the story (which I originally saw in the *New York Times* in October 2011 titled "A Silicon Valley School That Doesn't Compute") has become a hotly discussed topic . . . where else but online.

Can kids learn math better from a teacher than from an iPad? What good is an education if a child can't learn how to use a physical dictionary? You can see how the discourse evolves. Kids do not need Google, a great math teacher is much better than an iPad app, and it's important that kids know what an actual book is.

But there's something else we need to remember: Our values were created in a different time and in a different place. Let's rephrase the question: Am I doing my children a service or disservice by not allowing their education to include computers, technology, and connectivity? This is not a zero-sum game. Think about it this way: The jobs that the majority of my friends are currently working at didn't even exist as occupations when I was in high school. Should children be lugging around five textbooks in a backpack, or does an iPad give them not only a lighter load but also the ability to create, collaborate, and engage more with their peers (when used correctly)?

What do you see in the near future? Do you see a world of cubicles, desks, and paper clips, or do you see a very different world? While some may think it's important to keep technology away from our kids for as long as possible, I'd argue that it's not an all-or-nothing proposition. I can't imagine my kids ever using an HB pencil when they finally enter the workforce... in fact, I'm willing to bet that they won't even be using a keyboard and a mouse on a computer like we do today. So yes, history is important, but not more important than preparing children for the future.

Remember, if you don't keep up with the technology of today, there's not going to be much need for your professional services in the future. Reboot your life. Reboot your career.

That said, we all need to be a lot more careful about technology.

After attending the TED 2012 conference in Long Beach, California, I could not help but think about just how pervasive technology and media have become in our lives. If you could be in a room with over one thousand of the world's most interesting business leaders, thinkers, scientists, and artists, would you spend every free moment sitting in the corner alone thumbing your smartphone, or would you immerse yourself in the live experience and do your best to "press the flesh," as the saying goes?

Prior to the many sessions at TED 2012, the hosts would remind people to turn off their mobiles. It's become a ceremonial ritual at almost every conference, but in this instance, they took it a step further. The hosts didn't just ask us to set our phasers to vibrate; they demanded that we put them away and forget about them. In other words, in order for us to benefit from the discussion on new technology, they asked us to put away our own technology. Pretty ironic.

Is this what connections are really about?

Multiple speakers at TED questioned our connection to technology. Sherry Turkle questioned whether we're living in the here-and-now or living to create an impression for others of how we would like to be perceived. Thomas P. Campbell (director of the Metropolitan Museum of Art) wondered how digital media can be compared with spending real time in a museum. It didn't stop there. A theme of anti-Web sentiment (or a digital connectedness unplugging) was pervasive. Even Chip Kidd (famed book cover designer) pleaded for a return to the admiration of books in their dead-tree format. While we embrace technology and race forward with it, it seems like the past two decades have now culminated in what can only be described as a backlash to our connectivity.

It's true. We probably do spend too much time with technology and not enough time having meaningful conversations with others while looking them directly in the eyes. That said, it's not an all-or-nothing proposition either. I've heard many stories of troubled teens using platforms like Facebook to ask someone out or even ask for help because it allows them to feel more confident. I've heard stories of kids with disabilities leveraging social media to connect and then finding their school experience that much better because those with whom they had communicated online felt some kind of closer connection with them. Personally, some of my best friends are people I first met in the digital sense; because of shared values, we created much more powerful connections after either meeting in person or staying connected in a more personal way online.

Plus technology is very seductive. We love our iPhones and iPads. For many people, it's the last thing we stroke before we go to bed and the first thing we touch when we wake up in the morning. *We may not like it, but this is who we have become.* Next time you're in a public space, study the people around you. Notice how they flirt and caress their smartphones. It's bordering on sexual, isn't it? This isn't about getting rid of technology. It's about being conscious of our experiences.

Bear in mind that rich experiences don't happen via text messaging. Rich experiences happen when we're face-to-face, listening, sharing, and growing. Text messaging can be a great bridge between these very human experiences, but let's not kid ourselves into thinking that anything on your smartphone screen is as important as what's in front of your face. You don't have to unplug to become more human—you just have to make a choice. The future will be about more human and real choices.

THE NEXT #6—THE GOODS ON VIRTUAL GOODS.

While scaling and monetizing e-commerce is still an issue for many of the top brands in the world, those businesses should also keep an eye out for virtual goods. Brands and retailers need to spend some serious time focused on the opportunity that lies ahead with virtual goods.

Think about the current opportunity (and where this is all going). Why wouldn't a department store start selling digital versions of products like music, movies, and books? Why wouldn't those same stores sell subscription-like services to stream these types of media? Think about the opportunity to create multichannel marketing campaigns by offering up exclusives on things like unique levels in Angry Birds or new music from Gotye with either an online or in-store purchase. And this is only the beginning.

Some of the major retailers (like JCPenney and Target) are already embracing celebrity-endorsed brands, so why not extend this to the online/virtual goods channel? Imagine exclusive wallpapers for your iPad and/or iPhone designed by Demi Lovato and sold through her new relationship with Target. As Madonna and other stars line up to sell accessories through Macy's, virtual goods could provide an increasingly powerful opportunity to tie in exclusive physical and virtual goods to up the overall basket and bring the physical and the virtual worlds closer together.

We tend to think with extreme shortsightedness. The truth is that nobody can forecast the future of how people will buy, but as distribution gets more complex and the cost of building, maintaining, and staffing individual stores continues to rise, the businesses of the future are going to have to embrace the very real reality that consumers no longer draw a hard line between their virtual goods and their physical goods. Don't believe me? Look at the quick transition the mass public made from a physical CD of music to an iTunes library. Then along came the cloud and everything changed yet again.

While some of this may seem very technical and not relevant to your day-to-day work of trying to grow your business, the truth is that these new ways to access and interact with brands and content are creating some fundamental shifts in business. As the music industry continues to unravel and as the next generation of music business models evolve, the cloud is starting to weigh heavily on how we all connect to music. iTunes enabled all of us to buy music and store it on our hard drives, iPhones, and iPods. The ability to create playlists and organize our music has fundamentally changed how we buy and listen to music. Recently, services like Spotify and rdio have begun offering unlimited music everywhere. For a small monthly fee (usually under $10), you get access to a massive collection of music that can all be streamed from the cloud to almost any device that has Internet connectivity. So instead of choosing songs on iTunes, buying them, downloading and storing them, you can now simply stream everything from this massive collection. Think of it as a cable TV service for music.

Why own?

When I was given an evaluation license for Spotify and rdio, it quickly made me realize that even though my physical CD collection had already become digital, I had now developed a lack of desire to actually own any sort of data at all. This creates a compelling case for the power of the cloud and virtual goods. In other words, would I rather own a bunch of songs or have unlimited access to as much music as possible? Yes, both rdio and Spotify also allow users to buy and download music, but there just doesn't seem to be a point to physically owning the files (unless there are times when you're not connected to the Internet and want to listen to music—like on a plane or in an area that lacks connectivity).

As mobile data and Internet connectivity converge with faster speeds and more competitive pricing, everything is quickly moving to the cloud—from your business data to your home entertainment to new and interesting products and services to buy. This creates new businesses, new job opportunities, and much more innovation. But with that innovation also comes massive disruption. Yes...more disruption. This is a time of great upheaval in business. With that upheaval comes considerable opportunity for companies and individuals brave enough to see this as a once-in-a-lifetime chance to do something new and amazing in business.

Digitization is as digitization does.

While some industries are being forced into digitization (music, movies, books, software, etc.), your business doesn't have to be. You can take a leadership stance by embracing and encouraging the sale and distribution of more and more virtual goods. Initially, this will look much more like strategic partnerships (where a company like Warner Bros. would team up with a major retailer like Urban Outfitters to distribute their virtual goods), but it could (and should) lead to a point where your business will be developing your own merchandising team against virtual goods, and building that new category within your business.

Look no further than Apple to see a glimpse as to how this can play out (you buy your computer, iPod, or whatever at the retail level, then fill it up with content and software through their digital channel—iTunes). The brands of the future will be the ones that master both the physical and virtual development of goods and how they integrate their products with their services to become one holistic offering. This will produce business models that our world has yet to see.

AND IN THE END...

So what does it all mean? Well, let me let you in on a little secret of mine.

The truth is, I often think about the end of my life. I'm not ashamed to admit that I'm scared about how my life will end— and I don't want it to do so anytime soon. There are plenty more things that I want to accomplish in my life. I discovered (mostly through trial and error) that I love the marketing world. I love working with brands and thinking about brands and tinkering with what they can do to connect (more honestly and powerfully) with their consumers.

I'm writing this last part of the book on an airplane flight. I look around and I see people—from all walks of life—working in various occupations, and all of them are carrying a ton of technology with them. From smartphones and Kindles to iPads and laptops. I can't help but wonder and think about a time in the not-too-distant future when we're no longer carrying these devices around but they are actually in us...a part of us (sub-dermal implants or brain-activity-activated...who knows?). As I was walking through the airport, I noticed that the current cover story for *Wired* magazine is all about self-driving cars. Such instances of science fiction catching up to reality get me excited. They get me thinking more about how much I love business, and it makes me hopeful that I'll be privileged enough to be alive long enough to see how we innovate from this very powerful moment in time that we currently find ourselves in.

When I think about my career (or when I see other people thinking about their careers), it strikes me that even with goal set-ting and planning, it's usually a very shortsighted vision. Think about your current work situation. You're probably wondering about your next bonus or raise, your next step up the corporate ladder, or that new business pitch that is just around the corner. Maybe you're thinking about where you're going to be in the next five to ten years. But what about the end? *Ctrl Alt Delete* is a book about the evolution and reboot of business. It's also a book about the role that I want to have in it, and the role that I hope you would like to have in it as well. It made me realize that I only have one true goal for myself in the business world: *longevity*.

Longevity is key.

In looking back, it was always there, but it wasn't something that I was able to verbalize or acknowledge until very recently. *I want a business career with longevity.* Nothing less. In looking at the client work we do at Twist Image, this book, my writing on our blog, the weekly podcast that I create, my first book, *Six Pixels of Separation*, and many of the things that make up my personal work on a day-to-day basis—they're all about longevity.

How many people and businesses do you know that started a blog, a Facebook page, a LinkedIn community, or many other things that they simply dropped or got bored with? Yes, there's a moment in time when you have to ditch what's not working or even disengage if the channel can no longer deliver economic value to your brand, but in general, I think most brands have very shortsighted and short-term goals and visions. My blog has been around since 2003. I can recall saying to myself that the Internet gods have given me a great gift to be able to publish (and without editors telling me what's good or bad and without massive costs to reach an audience). Not only did I commit to it as a platform that fits with our business goals but I knew that I wanted it to have that longevity as well.

The same can be said of this book and what you do with it. Some of the statistics may be old by the time you read this. Some of the business cases may not have unfolded as I had hoped. Some of the businesses that I have written about may not even be in business anymore. That doesn't change the narrative of this story. Business has changed. Business continues to change. We are stuck in a moment of purgatory. What are you going to do? What does your reboot look like?

Longevity doesn't happen quickly. That doesn't mean I don't put a tremendous amount of focus on creating a sense of urgency in the work that I do (and I recommend that you do the same). I want to get great stuff done (and yes, I like quick wins as much as the next person). But when you're focused on longevity (for both yourself, professionally, and the brands you represent), odds are that you're going to do a lot more critical thinking. Ultimately, you will be putting things into the market with a much more solid foundation and expectation of good outcomes. I'm starting to think about everything in terms of longevity in these moments of purgatory, and the value that comes with it.

So . . . what are you after?

I wish you longevity.

Acknowledgments

A book is never the isolated thinking of just the author. It takes a village... or, more specifically in my case, a family. While I dedicated this book to my wife and children, my true co-author in this endeavor is my wife, Ali. She ensured that our very young children were (somewhat) away and quiet so Daddy could tap the keys on weekday evenings and, yes, even on weekends. There is no chance this book could have come together without Ali ensuring that our day-to-day family life maintained a level of normalcy, and I will be forever grateful to her for encouraging me to go and play with the kids—even when I was on deadline and stressing out. You were right, Ali (you always are)... it was worth it!

Mom and Dad have nothing but love and pride for everything that I do (they are master kvellers). Not only did they create me, but they were instrumental in getting me interested in all things media- and technology-related. How could you possibly find the words to thank parents like that? Thank you. Thank you. Thank you.

I said it in the acknowledgments for *Six Pixels of Separation*, but it bears repeating: I miss my Bubby and Zaida very much. I think about them daily, and I know that this book would have blown them away with pride and happiness.

Arn, Winn, Jerry, Marnie, Reesa, Jessie, Lianna, Noah, Rachel,

261

Jake, Rebecca, Lily, Beverley, Andre, Martine, Annabelle, Yahav, Jacques, Natalie, Ella, Maya, Ethan, Tristan, Olivia, Eva, Marcia (and the whole Shuster clan), and Sam—our family means the world to me, and your constant care, love, and support were instrumental in getting through this content to produce something that would make you all proud. I hope I did not let you down.

Mark Goodman, Mick Kanfi and Aubrey Rosenhek, every team member at Twist Image, and all of our amazing clients: This book is as much yours as it is mine. With every passing day, you all push me to be as creative and innovative as possible in thinking about digital and what it means to us as human beings. I'm fortunate to be surrounded by peers who—like me—want business to become more human and personal. The words on this page are the words we live with, hack, and tinker with each day. I'm very lucky to have you all in my life. You are my definition of success, and I consider myself one of the most successful people in the world because of our relationships.

I don't think that Dan Ariely knew what he was getting into when he first introduced me to his literary agent, James Levine. I don't have the words to express my gratitude to Dan for following through and actually making the introduction to Jim. That action alone speaks volumes about the level of integrity and kindness that is Dan Ariely (and if you haven't read his books *Predictably Irrational*, *The Upside of Irrationality*, and his latest, *The Honest Truth About Dishonesty*, you don't know what you're missing).

There are no greater literary agents than Jim Levine and his team at the Levine Greenberg Literary Agency. I often tell him that he's my business partner when I'm writing a book, and I mean it. Whether acting as a sounding board during the ideation phase or pushing back during the proposal writing, he is always a cool, calm, and collected professional who knows what it takes to write a bestselling business book. Whenever my thoughts are backed up against a wall, a quick call to Jim always puts them back on the right course. I hope we work together on many more books and projects for years to come.

Authors tend to talk smack about their publishers. There are usually few nice words. I don't know what I did to deserve a publisher like Rick Wolff and his amazing team at Business Plus and Hachette Book Group, but it must have been something incredibly kind. In short: Rick believes in me and how I see business. This makes our relationship incredibly close. He not only provides powerful editorial feedback but is amazing at helping me get things done. I'm forever thankful to be a part of the Business Plus imprint, and along with Jamie Raab and everyone at the publishing house, I hope we get to create many more volumes together.

I've had the fortune of working with Martin and Farah Perelmuter over at Speakers' Spotlight for over seven years. They believed in my content and presentation skills long before Twist Image was a popular agency and long before most people cared about my blog or books. Since then, I've spent years on the road connecting with audiences all over Canada because of them. Martin, Farah, and the entire team of Speakers' Spotlight are true angels. In an industry where talent agents have notoriously terrible reputations, Speakers' Spotlight is a bright light. I'm so thankful to everyone who works there for their tireless dedication in helping me get my ideas to spread.

Not that Martin and Farah have to worry about the competition, but Don Epstein, David Evenchick, and everyone at Greater Talent Network work equally as hard to book me all over the rest of the world. They welcome me with open arms every time I visit New York City, and do everything they can to ensure that the rest of the world is a stage for my presentations. They constantly and consistently deliver relevant events for me to speak at, and I do my best to never let them down once I'm up there. David and his team have my best interests at heart, and that makes them a complete pleasure to work with.

Chris Anderson, the TED team, and my fellow TEDsters. My first TED event was the last one held in Monterey. I've done my best to attend every TED since then. There are few events that rattle my brain and get me thinking more than TED. While billions of people have viewed the TED talks online, I often tell people that the presentations are a minor component of what makes TED so special. TED is more about the attendees and what happens in between the sessions than it is about the presentations. I'm sure many of the concepts and ideas I bring forward in *Ctrl Alt Delete* were formulated or percolated because of someone I met in a hallway at TED. I'm thankful for TED because—every year—it gives me a week to be extremely self-indulgent. TED is my personal time for me to learn and grow. Thanks, TED.

To everyone who is a part of the *Six Pixels of Separation* community, this book is not for you. Whether you read the blog regularly or listen to the weekly podcast, you are the ones who know this content, who live this content, and who breathe this content. Thank you for enduring my long words and weekly conversations with business leaders. I realize how much content I publish, and I recognize that it's not always easy to keep up with my frenetic pace. Thank you for keeping me honest. For correcting everything from simple grammar mistakes to conceptual thoughts that are still a little half baked. Please know that even though I may not respond to every blog comment, tweet, or Facebook message, I am reading and appreciating everything you contribute. Without you, I'm just writing a journal entry. With you, we are a movement of global citizens trying to make business better. Thank you!

An extra special thanks to Aubrey Rosenhek and Jaime O'Meara who took the time, energy, and effort to proofread everything.

Lastly, family, friends, business associates, and fellow community volunteers. The list is long and unwieldy, so I'm not even going to try to list everyone here. Ideas come from people, and the ideas in this book came from people just like you. Thank you for always being there, for always supporting my whims, and for helping me to find my muse.

Index

About the Author

When Google wanted to explain online marketing to the top brands in the world, they brought MITCH JOEL to the Googleplex in Mountain View, California. *Marketing* magazine dubbed him the "Rock Star of Digital Marketing" and called him "one of North America's leading digital visionaries." In 2006 he was named one of the most influential authorities on blog marketing in the world. Mitch Joel is president of Twist Image—an award-winning Digital Marketing and Communications agency (although he prefers the title Media Hacker). He has been called a marketing and communications visionary, interactive expert, and community leader. He is also a blogger, podcaster, passionate entrepreneur, and speaker who connects with people worldwide by sharing his marketing insights on digital marketing and new media. In 2008, Mitch was named Canada's Most Influential Male in Social Media, one of the top one hundred online marketers in the world, and was awarded the highly prestigious Canada's Top 40 Under 40. Most recently, Mitch was named one of iMedia's 25 Internet Marketing Leaders and Innovators in the world. *Marketing* magazine has named Twist Image one of the top ten agencies in Canada for two years running (and the only digital marketing pure-play to make the list).

Joel is a past chairman of the board of directors of the Canadian Marketing Association and a former board member of the

Interactive Advertising Bureau of Canada. He has been involved with the content committee for both Shop.org and the Web Analytics Association, and is on the advisory councils for many businesses and charitable organizations.

Joel speaks frequently to diverse groups like Walmart, Starbucks, Nestlé, Procter & Gamble, and Unilever, and has shared the stage with former president of the United States Bill Clinton, Sir Richard Branson, Malcolm Gladwell, Anthony Robbins, Tom Peters, and Dr. Phil. As a professional speaker, Mitch is represented exclusively by Greater Talent Network (Hachette Speakers Bureau) in the United States and by Speakers' Spotlight in Canada.

Prior to Twist Image, he co-launched Distort Entertainment, the only hard music label in Canada to have major label distribution (Universal Music) and whose roster features the platinum-plus, Juno Award– and MuchMusic Video Award–winning acts, Alexisonfire and City And Colour.

Joel is frequently called upon to be a subject matter expert for *BusinessWeek*, *Fast Company*, *Marketing* magazine, *Profit*, *Strategy*, *Money*, *The Globe and Mail*, and many other media outlets. He also has a regular column, "Media Hacker," on the *Huffington Post*. His first book, *Six Pixels of Separation* (published by Business Plus—Hachette Book Group), named after his successful blog and podcast, is a business and marketing bestseller.

You can visit Mitch's blog here: www.twistimage.com/blog

You can follow Mitch on Twitter here: @mitchjoel

Here's what people are saying about Mitch Joel online...

Want to observe a master at his trade? Watch @mitchjoel blog.

—Chris Brogan, @chrisbrogan

Who inspires you to be better at your job and in business—@mitchjoel hands down wins for me.

—Nathan Stower, @nathanstower

@mitchjoel This guy is one of the smartest marketers out there. He's cerebral and clever and a class act.

—Susan Baroncini-Moe, @suebmoe

@mitchjoel It was a delight to hear you speak. I learned so much...as always.   —Jim Kouzes, @Jim_Kouzes

Curious: Clay Shirky, Mitch Joel, and Seth Godin sport shaved pates, and they're all brilliant marketers. Conspiracy theory?

—Adam Daniel Mezei @TheRealADM

I just get smarter when I read @mitchjoel.

—John Jantsch, @ducttape

Think I'll pass along @mitchjoel's book to our CEO and COO when I'm finished. Content like that must be shared with the top.

—Jonathan Barrick, @j_barrick

One day @mitchjoel is going to be a household name. I told @sewlounge that this morning, and I believe it.

—Julien Smith, @julien

Mitch speaks all over the world to diverse groups like Walmart, Starbucks, Nestlé, Procter & Gamble, and has shared the stage with former President of the United States Bill Clinton, Sir Richard Branson, Malcolm Gladwell, and Tom Peters. If you would like to have Mitch show your company or group how to Ctrl Alt Delete your business, please contact the Hachette Speakers Bureau at 1-866-376-6591 or go to HachetteSpeakersBureau.com.